The Microbrew Lover's Cookbook

The Microbrew Lover's Cookbook

JAY HARLOW

SASQUATCH BOOKS
SEATTLE

Printed in the United States of America
Distributed by Publishers Group West
09 08 07 06 05 04 03 02   7 6 5 4 3 2 1

Cover and interior design and composition: Karen Schober
Copy editor: Rebecca Pepper
Proofreader: Sigrid Asmus

Library of Congress Cataloging in Publication Data
Harlow, Jay
The microbrew lovers' cookbook / Jay Harlow.
            p.   cm.
1. Cookery, International. 2. Beer. I. Title.

TX725.A1 H283 2002
641.59—dc21

Sasquatch Books
615 Second Avenue
Seattle, Washington 98104
(206) 467-4300
books@SasquatchBooks.com
http://www.SasquatchBooks.com

Contents

Recipes by Chapter

From the Beer Belt:
Beer and the Foods of Northern and Central Europe

Petites Gougères

Whisky-Cured Salmon with Whole-Grain Mustard Sauce

Mussels Steamed in Wheat Beer

Oysters on the Half Shell

Curried Beef Pasties

Pork Roast Stuffed with Prunes

Sweet and Sour Red Cabbage

Carbonnade of Beef Braised in Beer

Choucroute Garni des Brasseurs (Sauerkraut Braised with Assorted Meats)

Classic Standing Rib Roast

Individual Spinach Soufflés

Sauteed Chicken Breasts with Mushroom Sauce

Medallions of Venison with Currant Sauce

Cod Baked in Cider

Dungeness Crab au Naturel

Honey Cake with Stout

Pizza and Beyond:
Beer and the Foods of Mediterranean Europe

Tortilla Española

Squid Stuffed with Ham

Gambas al Ajillo (Garlic and Red Pepper Shrimp)

Salt Cod Crostini

Vegetable Antipasto Platter

Pizza

Focaccia

Cassoulet

Duck Confit

Rosemary-Crusted Rack of Lamb

Green Beans with Garlic Oil

Daube of Beef

Arroz con Pollo

Wild Mushroom Risotto

Summer Vegetable "Napoleon"

Penne with Broccoli, Garlic, and Bread Crumbs

Pasta with Sausage and Ricotta "Cream" Sauce

From the Spice Bazaar:
Beer and the Foods of North Africa, the Middle East, and India

Pappadams with Green Chutney

Kofta Kebab (Minced Lamb on Skewers)

Dolmas (Stuffed Grape Leaves)

Baba Ghanoush (Roasted Eggplant Dip)

Hummus

Pea Soup Avgolemono

Pomegranate Chicken

Rice Pilaf with Almonds

Lamb and Vegetable Tajine with Chickpea Couscous

Chicken Curry with Cashews

Naan (Tandoori-Style Flatbread)

Gobhi Bhaji (Pan-Fried Cauliflower with Spices)

Curried Winter Squash Soup

Beer in the Melting Pot:
Beer and American Regional Food

Spicy Chicken Wings

Crab Cakes with Chipotle Aioli

Warm Escarole Salad with Smoked Chicken

Grilled Salmon Sandwich

Grilled Eggplant Sandwich

Fish Baked in Beer Batter

Chili, My Way

Cheese and Beer Bread

Meat Loaf

Roasted Potato Wedges

Perfect Roast Chicken

Garlic Mashed Potatoes

Louisiana-Style Fish Courtbouillon

Muffuletta

Shrimp Boil

Pepper Slaw

Gingery Peach Crisp

Shrimp or Crawfish Étouffée

Cider-Brined Roast Stuffed Turkey with Giblet Gravy

Rye Bread and Apple Stuffing

Mixed Rice Jambalaya

Cranberry-Orange Relish

Leek and Potato Soup

Maggie Klein's Squash Gratin with Garlic and Olive Oil

INTRODUCTION: EAT GLOBALLY, DRINK LOCALLY

Not too many years ago, a North American beer drinker in search of flavorful, distinctive beers had to look overseas. When I came of legal drinking age in 1974, American beer was practically synonymous with one style: pale, light-tasting, crystal-clear lager, refreshing to drink on a hot day or with spicy foods. Typical Canadian beer was similar, if marginally more flavorful. With a few notable exceptions, the only beers that demonstrated the wider range of beer flavors and styles were imported, mostly from northern Europe and the British Isles.

What a change the last three decades have seen. The familiar pale, mass-market lagers brewed by a handful of giant brewing companies still dominate the North American beer market, and the selection of imported beers is larger than ever. But a third alternative has emerged, in the form of hundreds of smaller local and regional breweries. Among them, these small brewers manage to duplicate nearly every brewing style known in the Old World, as well as some distinctively New World varieties.

Nowhere has this change been more dramatic than in the region bordering the Pacific Coast (and, by a not too strained extension, the Rocky Mountain states). The region that gave birth to the "microbrewery" model in the mid-1970s remains the happiest place in the country to be a beer lover. The 1980s and '90s saw an explosion of new, mostly small breweries across America, but nowhere in greater numbers than in the West. Some of these breweries have been and gone, some have

consolidated, but many have remained as viable small businesses catering to a local trade. Others like Redhook, Sierra Nevada, and Pyramid
have outgrown the "microbrewery" category to become important
regional producers, to the point that they have attracted interest, imita-
tion, and in some cases investment from the big brewers.

Whatever the scale, these "micro-" or "craft" breweries have in common the vision of a new generation of brewers. Disappointed in the
bland sameness of beers brewed by the huge national brewing companies and exposed to more flavorful Old World models, these pioneers
have made it their business to bring back flavor and diversity to American beers. Together, they have revolutionized North American brewing,
reviving some traditional styles of beer and ale and developing a few
new ones. (There is no Old World equivalent of Anchor Liberty Ale or
Alaskan Smoked Porter, to name a couple.)

All in all, the new generation of brewers is providing us with better
and more varied beer than ever. Nearly every city has several pubs featuring an assortment of fine beers and ales on tap, and most have one or
more brewpubs making their own beer on the premises. It all comes
down to more choice for beer drinkers. You can still find Guinness
Stout on tap in plenty of places, but chances are they are also pouring
another stout brewed a few miles away rather than shipped halfway
around the world.

The new role of beer in the West did not occur in a vacuum; it's gone
hand in hand with changes in everything we eat and drink. The West
Coast has led the nation in interest in (some would say obsession with)
our food—how it is produced, how it is distributed, and above all, how
it tastes. Consumers continue to demand more flavor, more freshness,
and more natural ingredients in everything from salad greens, bread,
and cheese to coffee and beer. We are also becoming more attuned to
the seasons, and to balancing our desire for ingredients from around the
world with supporting our local farmers, fishermen, and yes, brewers.

The other great trend in West Coast food and drink over recent
decades can be seen in the sheer variety of our food tastes, as travel and
immigration continue to add new flavors to our collective food vocabu-
lary. Here on the western edge of North America, the way people cook
and eat today represents a mingling of food traditions from around the
world, with especially strong influences from Mediterranean, Asian,
Latin American, and regional American cuisines. New arrivals not only

assimilate North American traditions, but also those of their immigrant neighbors, and we are all the richer as we grow up increasingly familiar with each other's food. Shopping for ingredients to recreate the flavors we encounter in restaurants and homes, we find not only more imported items, but more being grown and produced here, from lemongrass and Asian pears grown in Washington to balsamic vinegar and Thai-style *sriracha* sauce made in California.

Whether you call this blending of flavors and traditions "eclectic," "New American," "fusion," "Pacific Rim cuisine," or give it some other label, I think it's no coincidence that a lot of our favorite foods go very well with beer. In a sense, modern West Coast cooking and modern West Coast beer have grown up together, like the local food and drink in much of the Old World. It's a relationship summed up in the title of this introduction, which might just as well be the title of the book.[1]

While the focus of this book is on local brews, I am not suggesting that we should stop drinking imported beers. Staying familiar with the world's classic beer styles gives us all important benchmarks as our homegrown styles continue to evolve. Those who make and enjoy wine, cheese, and other artisan foods would be fools to turn their backs on the best that the Old World has to offer, and the same goes for beer.

Throughout this book I refer to various styles of beer and specific examples of beers I like and consider typical of those styles. However, I do not consider myself a beer expert, just an aficionado. You may well disagree with my classification of XYZ Ale as a Brown Ale rather than a Porter, let alone whether it represents a particularly good example of either. If you prefer another, by all means enjoy it.

I probably shouldn't worry; most beer drinkers are far too sensible to let anyone else tell them what to drink. Instead, I hope this book will encourage you to explore some new cuisines and consider some new ideas on pairing foods and beers. I also hope that you will find some favorite new recipes for dishes to enjoy with your favorite beers. If that happens, I will consider the book a success.

Jay Harlow

1. *I am well aware (as I assume are many readers) of the brilliant phrase of French environmentalist René Dubos, who in 1972 advised us to "think globally, act locally" on environmental issues. I believe this advice is as important today as it was thirty years ago, and I certainly do not mean to trivialize it by adapting his construction to a quite different context. If anyone is offended, I apologize.*

BREWING IN THE WEST

Beer and brewing have been part of American history since the first arrival of English, and later Dutch, settlers in the Northeast. (Few beer writers can resist quoting the log of the *Mayflower*, which landed in Massachusetts rather than heading on to Virginia, "our victuals being much spente, especially our beere.") Along with cider and rum, beer was one of the standard beverages in colonial America, with much of it made in the home; commercial brewing was limited to cities and larger towns.

Well into the nineteenth century, virtually all American beer was ale, just as in the Old World. The introduction of lager brewing from Europe in the 1840s (see Chapter 2) led to a revolution in both the style and quantity of American beer. As the United States expanded westward, lager brewers, almost all of them German, set up shop wherever they could find good water, a source of ice (a necessity until the invention of mechanical refrigeration and ice-making in the 1880s), and a thirsty population. The latter half of the nineteenth century saw the rise of the pale, golden, effervescent style of lager and the brewing companies (among them Anheuser-Busch, Miller, Schlitz, Pabst, Coors, and in the Northwest, Blitz-Weinhard, Rainier, and Olympia) that would define American beer for the next hundred years.

Consolidation of the brewing industry was well under way when the U.S. adopted a national ban on the "manufacture, sale, or transportation of intoxicating liquors" in 1920. The 18th Amendment was preceded by many years of increasing local, county, and state restrictions, including statewide prohibition in Oregon and Washington starting in 1916.

Many smaller breweries never reopened after Prohibition, and the consolidation of the industry continued through the middle third of the twentieth century. By the 1970s it looked like there would soon be nothing but three or four look-alike, taste-alike beers left, and beer drinkers in search of something more distinctive or flavorful looked mainly to imported beers. Most began with Heineken, available just about everywhere and having a sharper touch of bitterness than American lager. Better-stocked stores and bars carried some other European lagers like Löwenbräu (still coming from Munich then), the Danish Carlsberg and Tuborg, and genuine Pilsner Urquell from Czechoslovakia.

Those who had been to England came back talking about pints of amber-colored ale, rich in taste even if they were mysteriously served warm and flat. Back home they would seek out Bass Ale in bottles, or on tap in British-style pubs. The ultimate beer in those days was Guinness Stout, so flavorful it was sold in packages of four bottles where other beers came in six-packs.

There were a few local beers that offered distinctive flavor. Seattle's Rainier Ale, known to its loyal fans and detractors alike as "the Green Death," was a pale amber beer with good body, a noticeable hop bite, and a perception of great strength. Anchor Steam Beer, a San Francisco brand revived in the 1960s, was a copper-colored beer as hoppy and rich as an English bitter.

From time to time beginning in the early 1970s, the major brewers would test more flavorful beers on European models or resurrect some defunct local brand name, but most of these experiments either faded back into bland sameness or disappeared. Meanwhile, a growing number of frustrated beer drinkers (especially in northern California and the Pacific Northwest) turned to brewing their own beers and ales, using older recipes and considerably more malt and hops than the big commercial breweries. Home brewing was an underground phenomenon until it was officially legalized in 1976, after which homebrew clubs and shops mushroomed. Some of these home brewers eventually turned their efforts to small-scale commercial brewing, and the "microbrewery" revolution was born.

The first "micro" in the country, New Albion in Sonoma, California, opened in 1976 and lasted only until 1980. Within a couple of years of its demise, other pioneering micros, including Sierra Nevada, Bert Grant's Yakima Brewing & Malting, Buffalo Bill's Brewpub, and Mendocino Brewing (the last using some of New Albion's equipment), had begun operations, and they were soon joined by Redhook of Seattle and others. By 1991, the third edition of Michael Jackson's *Pocket Guide to Beer* listed more than 80 small to medium-size breweries in California, Oregon, Washington, British Columbia, and Alaska, and another 30 or so in other western states and provinces.

With few exceptions, the West Coast homebrew and microbrew boom has been dominated by ale brewing. Ales in general are easier to produce, requiring less time and space than slower-fermenting lagers. Many West Coast brewers were also influenced by the British CAMRA (Campaign for Real Ale) movement of the 1970s, which worked to maintain and revive traditional ale styles against the increasing standardization of British beers (and the growing popularity of lager). However, there have always been some craft brewers who looked to Germany rather than the British Isles for models, and Thomas Kemper in Washington (now a brand of Pyramid) and Sudwerk and Gordon Biersch in California have bucked the trend by concentrating on lagers. Belgian ale styles continue to grow in popularity; Colorado's New Belgium Brewing has a Belgian brewer and a full product line based on Belgian styles, while many other breweries have dabbled in Belgian-style brews.

At the beginning of the microbrewery movement, federal and state laws did not allow businesses to both brew beer and serve it, so early microbreweries generally sold all their beer in kegs to be served on draft in local pubs or bottled it for sale through local wholesale channels (sometimes both). However, a change in the law in 1982 allowed the birth of the brewpub, a place that serves beer brewed on the premises, usually with food as well.

By the early 1990s, the brewpub concept was crossing over into higher-ticket restaurants, and for a while it seemed that a six-barrel brewing system was as much a requisite for a new restaurant as a mesquite grill or a wood-burning pizza oven. Some of these were individual operators, lured by the promise of turnkey systems that could convert a few cents' worth of ingredients into a $3 pint of beer, and many have gone by the wayside. Chain and franchise operations based on solid business plans have proven more reliable, and there are several such groups operating around the country.

Of course, the vast majority of restaurants are not brewing their own beer, but by and large the restaurant world has woken up to the fact that some diners prefer beer, even in a white-tablecloth setting. While few offer a beer list with anywhere near the depth of their wine lists, most are realizing that their beer-drinking customers won't settle for just one or two obvious choices. Chances are they have a tap or two serving craft-brewed (preferably locally brewed) beers.

Specialty and microbrew beers have also become more common in small ethnic restaurants. It used to be that the choice with Thai, Vietnamese, Mexican, Korean, or other ethnic cuisine was limited to a couple of beers from the home country plus Heineken, Bud, and a "light" beer; but in recent years the distributors of regional craft brewers like Sierra Nevada, Anchor, and Redhook have made major inroads into the small restaurant market, and some also feature genuine microbrews from local breweries.

Eleven years ago, in my previous book on this subject, I wrote "There has never been a better time than now to be a beer lover, especially in America." That is even more true today, especially here on the Pacific Coast, and I see no reason why it won't continue to improve in the years to come.

THE BREWING 2 PROCESS

Beer, in the most general sense, is a mildly alcoholic beverage made from a fermented liquid extract of grains. Unlike winemaking, which is keyed to an annual harvest cycle, brewing is largely an "anytime" process, in which a given type of beer can be made by recipe, when and where the brewer wants. All beers are produced by more or less the same process, but minor differences along the way make all the difference in flavor, aroma, color, strength, and other attributes of individual beers and styles.

The following is a rough guide to the brewing process; more specifics are discussed elsewhere in the book in the profiles of various brewing styles. Some of the terms are defined in the Glossary of Brewing and Tasting Terms on page 7. But the best way to learn about the brewing process is to take a brewery tour; most brewers both large and small love to talk about the intricacies of their craft, offering samples of the results.

The basic ingredients of beer are water (up to 95 percent of the finished product), barley (and sometimes other grains), hops, and yeast, all of which are readily available to West Coast brewers. Most of the West was settled near sources of water, particularly the soft, neutral runoff from rain and snow that falls on the Cascades, Sierra Nevada, and other West Coast mountains. A lot of the barley used here is locally grown, although some brewers prefer the flavors of imported grain.

While they make up a relatively small portion of the recipe, hops are an essential part of beer. The aromatic dried blossoms of a perennial vine native to central Europe, hops contain a complex blend of essential oils, acids, and tannins that give a distinctive aroma and refreshing bitterness to most beer. Several places in the Pacific Northwest, especially the semiarid region east of the Cascades, turn out to have ideal soil and climate for hops, making this the largest hop growing region outside Europe. Perhaps coincidentally, perhaps not, West Coast brewers are among the world's most enthusiastic in the use of hops.

The first step in making beer, **malting,** usually takes place in a separate facility from the brewery. While it is possible to make beer from unmalted grains, malting converts barley to a form in which much more of the carbohydrates are available for fermentation. Roasting the malt stops the germinating process, which would otherwise turn the grains into green sprouts, and dries the malted grains so they can be stored without spoiling. Equally important, the degree of roast determines the color and flavor of the malt, from pale golden to almost black.

In the first step in the brewery, **mashing,** crushed malt grains are combined with warm water in a large vessel called the mash tun. In a few hours, the water dissolves the maltose, as well as small amounts of protein and other carbohydrates. The choice and combination of malts, from pale golden through various shades of brown to nearly black, determines the color and flavor of the resulting liquid, called **wort,** and whether the final beer will be a delicate, pale golden lager, a thick, blackish stout, or anything in between.

After filtering, the wort goes into a brew kettle for the actual **brewing,** in which the wort is boiled with hops to destroy any remaining enzymes or spoilage organisms and to extract the flavor of the hops. Brewers can select among dozens of varieties of hops, some with more bittering power, others especially aromatic. Because much of the aroma of the hops is lost in boiling, brewers sometimes add more hops at the end of the brewing stage.

From the brew kettle, the wort is strained again and rapidly cooled (sometimes using an intercooler that warms the next batch of wort) to the proper temperature for **fermentation.** The brewer introduces a carefully cultivated strain of yeast, a single-celled fungus which grows rapidly in the wort, feeding on the sugar and converting it to ethyl alcohol and carbon dioxide. Here again, the brewer has choices to make: for ales, to ferment at warm cellar temperature with "top-fermenting" yeasts (so called because they form a thick, foamy mat on the surface of the liquid), or for lagers, to ferment at colder temperatures with a different variety of yeast that remains suspended throughout the wort and is known as "bottom-fermenting."

Early in the fermentation process, the carbon dioxide is allowed to escape, but at a certain point the brewer may seal the fermentation vessel so the gas stays dissolved in the beer. Others prefer to let the beer ferment to nearly flat, than reintroduce the CO_2 under pressure to reach the desired level of carbonation.

Over the next few days (up to two weeks in the case of lagers), the yeast cells consume the sugar, then gradually die off for lack of food and settle to the bottom of the vessel. At this point the beer is transferred to another container for a resting or **conditioning** period. Ales are generally ready for consumption after just a few days, while lagers (which take their name from a German word meaning to store) are held for at least two weeks at near-freezing before being packaged. After a final filtering (omitted in some cases, such as hefeweizens and "cask-conditioned" ales), the beer is put into bottles or kegs for sale. With a few exceptions, beer is at its best as soon after packaging as possible, and should be enjoyed within weeks or at most a few months.

Glossary of Brewing and Tasting Terms

ADJUNCTS Grains and other sources of fermentable sugars other than barley or wheat. Adjuncts such as corn or corn sugar, rice, and cane sugar can reduce the cost of brewing, but generally diminish flavor. Common in North American mass-market beers, rarely used in craft brewing.

ALCOHOL BY VOLUME The most common measure of alcoholic strength in beer (and other beverages) worldwide, sometimes abbreviated ABV on labels. U.S. laws used to specify beer strength in alcohol by weight; since alcohol is lighter than water, this gave lower apparent levels, and led to the widespread misconception that standard American beer is weaker than imported beers. Most beers worldwide range from 4 to 5 percent ABV (3.2 to 4 percent by weight). West Coast craft beers tend to be slightly stronger, in the 5 to 6 percent range, and many seasonal beers are stronger still.

ALE One of the two basic styles of beer, fermented at relatively warm temperatures (65 to 68°F) with top-fermenting yeast. Characterized by fruity, **estery** flavors and aromas in addition to hops and malt. Compare **lager.**

ALTBIER Literally "old beer"; used in certain German regions with traditions of brewing ale rather than lager, and by a few Western brewers making beers in a similar style.

ASTRINGENT Causing a drying, tightening sensation to the mouth, especially the gums; imparted to beer by hops. Astringency is generally a positive, refreshing trait, unless it's too pronounced.

BARLEY Grain most typically used to brew beer. Barley grains must be converted to malt for most brewing.

BARLEY WINE The strongest category of ales (8 to 12 percent alcohol by volume), usually fairly sweet, and intended for sipping in small quantities with or as dessert. Long fermentation with multiple strains of yeast required to reach higher alcohol levels provides especially complex and fruity flavors and aromas.

BEER In the broadest sense, covers the whole range of fermented grain beverages. As used here, a category that encompasses lager, ale, and wheat beer.

BITTER 1. One of the five basic flavors, in beer associated mainly with **hops.** 2. An English ale style that, despite the name, is usually less bitter than pale ale. Produced by some West Coast brewers.

BOCK A style of lager, usually high-**gravity** lager, from Bavaria, traditionally brewed for spring consumption.

BODY The density or "mouth-filling" sensation of a beer, contributed mostly by alcohol and **dextrins.**

BOTTOM-FERMENTING Describes the kind of yeast used in **lager** fermentation, which remains suspended throughout the fermenting wort and gradually settles to the bottom. Compare with **top-fermenting.**

BREWERY A place where beer is brewed.

BREWING Strictly speaking, the stage of boiling **wort** and hops together prior to fermentation; more loosely, covers the entire process of producing beer from the time the malt and water are first combined through **fermentation** and **conditioning.**

BREWPUB An American term for an establishment where beer is brewed and served on the same premises; sometimes food is served as well.

BROWN ALE An English ale style, typically malty, medium-bodied, and slightly sweet with moderate hop flavor. West Coast examples are often more highly hopped than a typical English brown ale.

BUTTERY, BUTTERSCOTCH Describes the aroma of diacetyl, an organic compound produced by yeasts under certain temperature and chemical conditions during fermentation. A slight buttery aroma is an appreciated characteristic of certain styles of ale, but butteriness is considered a fault in other beers.

CASK-CONDITIONED Refers to beers, usually ales, that are transferred to small, portable barrels for final **conditioning**. Depending on the amount of sugar remaining in the wort, this final stage produces more or less natural carbonation as the carbon dioxide produced by fermentation remains dissolved in the beer.

CONDITIONING A resting stage after the most active phase of fermentation, during which the yeast cells gradually die for lack of sugar and settle to the bottom of the vessel, clarifying the beer. See **cask-conditioned, kräusening.**

CRAFT BREWERY A term preferred by some to **microbrewery** for an approach that is independent of size. Implies a traditional approach, in particular all-malt brewing without the use of **adjuncts.**

DEXTRINS Large-chain sugars produced in small quantities in the malting process; largely unfermentable by yeast, they remain in the beer, providing sweetness and **body.**

DUNKEL "Dark" in German; used for medium to dark brown lagers, often with a sweetish malt flavor.

ESTERY Having aromas suggesting fruits (especially banana or apple) or wine. Esters are a large class of aromatic organic compounds found naturally in fruits and formed in fermentation, especially the warm fermentation typical of ale brewing. Estery aromas are typical of most ale styles but are rare in lagers.

FERMENTATION A large class of organic chemical reactions. In beer terms, refers to the chemical process by which yeast cells feed on sugars, producing ethyl alcohol and carbon dioxide as by-products.

FRUITY See **estery.**

GRAVITY Short for original gravity, a measure of the amount of sugar in the **wort.** Since sugar converts directly to alcohol in fermentation, original gravity is an accurate predictor of final alcohol content.

HEFEWEIZEN A style of **wheat beer** that is not filtered after fermentation, so some spent yeast remains in the bottle or barrel and is intended to be consumed along with the beer.

HOPS The most common "seasoning" ingredient in beer. Hop cones, the flowers and surrounding leafy structures (bracts) of a tall-growing vine, are used in beer brewing to impart aroma, bitter flavor, and a natural preservative effect.

IMPERIAL STOUT A style of high-gravity **stout,** originally brewed by British brewers for export to the Russian court.

INDIA PALE ALE A variant of **pale ale** originating in nineteenth-century England, with both higher gravity and a higher level of hops to help preserve it on sea journeys to India and other far-flung colonies. A very popular style with West Coast brewers (often abbreviated IPA on labels).

KRÄUSENING Also known as bottle-conditioning. Beers bottled when some sugar and yeast remain in the wort will complete their fermentation in the bottle, trapping the carbon dioxide to provide natural carbonation. See **conditioning, cask-conditioning.**

LAGER One of the two basic styles of beer, fermented at relatively cold temperatures (45° to 50°F) with **bottom-fermenting** yeast and aged for several weeks to several months at similar temperatures (lager is German for "store"). Characterized by crystal clarity and straightforward flavors and aromas of malt and hops. Compare **ale.**

MÄRZEN, MÄRZENBIER Also spelled Maerzen. From German for "March beer"; a style of lager, usually amber in color and slightly stronger than a brewery's standard lager, brewed in spring and aged over the summer to be served at Oktoberfest. Brewed and sold year-round by several Western brewers.

MALT Barley or wheat that has been moistened and allowed to germinate; in the process, enzymes in the grain convert the relatively unfermentable starch into mostly fermentable sugars, primarily maltose. Roasting the malt dries the sprouted grains, deactivating the enzymes and making the malt storable for months. The temperature and duration of roasting determine the color and flavor of the malt, producing various types from pale to black.

MICROBREWERY Not a precisely defined term, but a brewery that produces on a smaller scale than a regional or national brewery.

MILD An English ale style, less highly hopped than **bitter.** Used as a style label by some West Coast brewers.

OKTOBERFEST A Bavarian festival season beginning in September; as a beer style, see **Märzen.**

PALE ALE An English ale style, usually some shade of reddish amber, "pale" only in comparison to darker ales like brown, porter, and stout. A very popular West Coast style, usually with a pronounced hop flavor and aroma.

PILSNER, PILSENER The archetype of pale lager, originally from the Czech city of Pilsen (Pilzn), it is pale golden with a pronounced hop aroma and softly malty flavor. Most domestic mass-market Pilsners are faint imitations of the original, but some West Coast brewers make a credible version.

PORTER Dark brown to nearly black ales in the English style, based on highly roasted malts; local examples vary widely but are usually dry and fairly bitter. See **stout.**

PUB British term, short for "public house," a place where beer and other drinks are sold. In this country, often implies a place more brightly lit and family-friendly than "bar." See **brewpub.**

SKUNKY Describes an aroma like that of a skunk, caused by a reaction of sulfur compounds in beer exposed to light. Especially common in beers sold in green or other pale-colored bottles. Sometimes called "light-struck," always a flaw.

STOUT The darkest ale style, dark brown to opaquely black, generally darker and fuller-bodied than **porter** (the original name for this style was stout porter). Local examples may be dry in the Irish style or sweet in the English tradition.

TOP-FERMENTING Describes the kind of yeast used in ale fermentation, which forms a thick mat on the surface of the fermenting wort. Compare with **bottom-fermenting.**

WEISS German for "white"; used for certain **wheat beers.**

WEIZEN German for "wheat"; see **wheat beer.**

WHEAT BEER Beer brewed with malted wheat in place of some or all of the barley.

WIT Flemish for "white"; a Belgian style of pale wheat beer flavored with coriander seed and orange peel.

WINTER WARMER A general name, sometimes a label term, for **high-gravity** beers brewed for cold-weather consumption.

WORT A solution of malt and water prior to and during fermentation into beer. See page 6.

YEAST A class of one-celled fungi. Beer yeasts (*Saccharomyces* spp.) ferment malt and other sugars by feeding on the sugar molecules, producing ethyl alcohol and carbon dioxide as by-products.

BEER AT THE TABLE:

Combining Beer and Food

Beer is a delicious, refreshing beverage on its own, but this book is about enjoying beer with food. While you can't go far wrong drinking beer you like with foods you like, some combinations are bound to be better than others.

The pleasure of matching beer and food, like that of pairing wine and food, begins with attention to the sometimes subtle differences among beers. Professional beer tasters can identify dozens of flavor components, from hop and malt varieties to compounds often present in minute amounts, that give each beer its unique flavor and aroma, and they use these flavor breakdowns to rate beers against established style standards. The rest of us may not be able to spot or name all the things that make our favorite beers taste the way they do, but it's clear that paying attention to their features can enhance our enjoyment of them. Whether or not you keep formal tasting notes, trying to describe what you like or don't like about a beer helps you focus better on both the beers and your own taste.

Tasting beer begins with looking at the beer in the glass. Depending on the style, the color may be anywhere in the spectrum from pale straw through shades of gold, amber, brown, or black. The head may be non-existent, thin and quick to disappear, or thick and long-lasting. Before you sip, take a sniff and enjoy the aroma. Look for a floral aroma of hops, sweetish aromas that may suggest caramel, toasty, or even burnt overtones, as well as chocolate or coffee aromas. Depending on the style, you may find fruity, spicy, or winy aromas as well. Take a sip; notice the initial taste impression, the middle flavors that develop, and the finish or aftertaste after you swallow. Notice the body (the "weight" on the palate), the balance of sweet and bitter flavors, the amount of carbonation, and the changes as the flavor fades away.

Finding the Balance

The first measure of a match of good beer and food is the balance of flavors. At least two thousand years ago, the Chinese identified a system of five flavors: sweet, sour, salty, bitter, and "pungent" or hot.[1] It's a system that still works very well in analyzing why certain flavor combinations work better than others. The best combinations of food and beverage contain all of these elements in balance, and a drastic imbalance is apt to show either the food or the drink in a worse light.

Certain flavors act to reduce an excess of others: sweet balances hot and sour; salt reduces the perception of sweetness; both hot and sour balance sweet and salty; bitter offsets sweet. Other combinations are relatively neutral, but sour flavors can intensify hot or bitter flavors.

Balance in flavor terms does not mean that all the elements are there in equal proportion. It may take just a small amount of a bitter, sour, salty, or sweet flavor to bring an otherwise one-dimensional dish into balance, and that amount may be barely perceptible. A chocolate chip cookie that tastes salty is all wrong, but one made without enough salt tastes flat. And the chocolate chips themselves combine bitter and sweet in a delicious way that is missing from the same cookie made with white chocolate.

In the five-flavor system, beer mainly contributes bitter and sweet flavors, and in a few styles a bit of sour acid. (Salty and hot do not enter the equation from the beer side, except in silly exercises like chile-flavored beers.) Beers also have some important components that affect the flavor of foods, including alcohol and the tannins in the hops. Like the tannins in tea, unsweetened chocolate, or red wine, hop tannins contribute an astringent effect, a drying and shrinking of the gums that also cuts through the film of fat left by rich foods. Let's look at how these elements work in good and bad combinations with foods.

Salty foods stimulate thirst, and many of the obvious "beer foods"—such as chips, pretzels, processed nuts, and pickles—are mostly salty. Whether they became standard beer companions because of a natural

1. There has always been some argument over whether pungent/hot is a true flavor or a separate physical sensation. The four other primary flavors—sweet, sour, salty, and bitter—each have identifiable taste receptors on the tongue, but the heat of chiles and other spices, like the astringency of tannin, is a more general, tactile sensation.

Some academics and chefs have proposed a fifth (sixth?) primary flavor, variously called "savory" and "a taste of fullness." The Japanese even have a word for it: umami. Foods considered high in umami, including ripe fruits and vegetables and fresh shellfish as well as ripened,

affinity or a cynical attempt to sell more beer, the fact is that something salty invites a sip of beer. At the same time, sip after sip of beer, with the sweet and mildly bitter flavors, can get monotonous, and a nibble of something salty keeps the palate interested.

Most of us don't eat a lot of simply sour foods; there's not much appeal to chomping on a slice of lemon or sipping straight vinegar. Usually sour flavors combine with others, like salty (pickles, preserved lemons), sweet (fruit and tomato sauces, ketchup, and many other condiments), or hot (chile salsas and other hot condiments). Drinking beer with foods like these offers a little more sweetness to cut the acidity, as well as a touch of bitterness to keep the palate fresh.

Bitterness in foods can get tricky when you add beer. A lot of spices and herbs have a bitter component to their flavor, but they are generally used only in small amounts. Where a bitter vegetable like watercress, mustard greens, or broccoli raab is a dominant part of a dish, I don't want an especially bitter beer. One with more emphasis on malt than hops is likely to be a better bet. (On the other hand, a compound in artichokes leaves an effect on the palate that makes whatever you taste next seem sweeter; a sip of beer along with an artichoke dish may taste startlingly sweet.)

With really sweet foods, beer doesn't have much to offer. Like coffee or port, very rich, winy-tasting barley wine or Imperial stout can go well with chocolate or not-too-sweet puddings, but in general when the dessert comes out I either finish off the last of my beer or put it aside for later.

Which leaves hot foods, one of the obvious partners to beer but also one of the more troublesome. The heat from chiles, pepper, ginger, and other spices actually creates a low level of pain in the mouth, which is relieved to a certain extent by any liquid. A little sugar also helps soothe a burning palate, and the slight malty sweetness in the middle flavor of most beers fills the bill nicely. Where the trouble comes is in the assumption by a lot of writers, chefs, and beer drinkers that you need a full-flavored (which usually means highly hopped) beer to "stand up to" a dish with a lot of hot flavors. I find just the opposite: Beyond a certain moderate level of both hops and chile, the bitter, astringent quality of hops amplifies the heat of chiles rather than balancing it. Higher alcohol also increases this effect, and bigger beers tend to be a little higher in alcohol as well. Ironically, the typical microbrewed India pale ale is

aged, and fermented foods ranging from aged cheeses to Southeast Asian fish sauce, contain high amounts of l-glutamate, the free form of an amino acid that has recently been shown to stimulate separate taste receptors from the other four flavors. Perhaps the most purely umami ingredient is the widely used but controversial mon-osodium glutamate (MSG), used to "enhance" other flavors in food. A number of chefs have begun to incorporate umami into their concepts of balancing flavors in a dish. I wonder if glutamate/umami has a role in evaluating beer flavor.

one of the worst choices to go with a hot Indian curry! A softer, maltier brew, like a brown or amber ale, works better for me.

Beyond balancing the five flavors, some beers can add flavors and aromas that add to the overall flavor mix. Besides contributing an appetizing aroma and bitter flavor, hops add some herbal flavor. Fruit- or spice-flavored beers are another obvious possibility. "Echoing" flavors between the beer and the food may sound like a good idea, but I wouldn't serve a fruited beer with a dish or a sauce containing fruit. The same goes for smoked-malt beers; they are often suggested to accompany smoked meats or fish, but I don't think the combination does much for either one. However, I won't let this principle get in the way of serving spiced beers with Thanksgiving dinner and other holiday meals (see page 223); with so many sweet-spicy flavors going on, the more the merrier.

Beer in the Kitchen

Only a very few recipes in this book call for beer as an ingredient. Plenty of books and articles have been written on cooking with beer, and I can understand the desire of brewpubs and oversupplied homebrewers to make distinctive dishes featuring their own brews. But for me, beer has a very limited role in cooking. Like wine, or for that matter rosemary, Parmesan cheese, balsamic vinegar, and sun-dried tomatoes, it can be a useful ingredient in certain contexts, but there is no reason to assume it will automatically improve any dish.

Where beer is to be used in cooking, it's important to choose carefully. Cooking with beer generally means boiling it down, which concentrates its flavors. If the beer has a lot of hop bitterness—and if there is one generalization that can be made about West Coast craft beers, it is that they are almost all generously hopped—the resulting sauce can be quite bitter. It's a good idea to taste the beer you are planning to cook with, and perhaps to try several varieties of the same style, to find the right one.

FROM THE BEER BELT:

Beer and the Foods of Northern and Central Europe

While some form of beer is brewed in many parts of the world, most if not all of the world's great beer styles originated in a thousand-mile-long stretch of Europe north and northwest of the Alps, from Bohemia to Ireland. To get an idea of the influence of this "beer belt," try to imagine brewing (or tasting) beer without any reference to Czech Pilsner, German lagers and weizenbiers in all their shades, Dutch and Danish lagers, the many-faceted Belgian wheat and abbey beers, English and Scottish ales, or Irish stout—what's left?

Beer as we know it grew up in this region because of its geography. The climate of northern and central Europe is too cold to grow grapes, except in the most favored microclimates, but it's well suited to growing barley and wheat. It's only natural that these grains became the base for everyday fermented beverages, although apples have an important role as well (see page 46).

The beer-belt countries also supplied most of North America's European population, at least until the mid-nineteenth century. Many of the foods familiar to North Americans of English, Scottish, Irish, and Germanic descent reflect the foodways of their ancestors. Sausages and other cured meats, cold-water seafoods, and dairy products are common across all northern European cuisines. Staple vegetables include potatoes, cabbage, root vegetables, and other hardy crops. Beer-belt cuisines are also characterized by braising, stewing, sweet and savory baked dishes, and (with notable exceptions) a light hand with spices. Beer sometimes becomes an ingredient, but not as often as you might guess.

Not surprisingly, the recipes in this chapter can go with a wide range of beers. I have noted my favorite pairings, but do follow your own tastes.

Espresso by the Pint: Stouts and Porters

It's no surprise that the region that spawned Peet's, Starbucks, and other purveyors of dark-roasted, flavorful coffee also brews a lot of full-flavored ales based on dark to black malt. When the early home-brewers and microbrewers were looking to make something with more flavor than the typical American beer, they naturally gravitated to the other end of the spectrum, Ireland's Guinness Stout. Around the same time, English brewers were beginning to resurrect porter, a somewhat lighter nineteenth-century London style that had become nearly extinct. Porters and various styles of stout remain favorites in English and Irish Pubs.

Irish stout generally has a dry finish, while English stouts can be quite sweet. Variations on the style include stouts with some oatmeal, milk, or even oyster extract added to the wort.

Drawing on these inspirations and more, West Coast brewers have developed many instant classics, including Deschutes Black Butte Porter, Sierra Nevada Porter, Anchor Porter, Rogue Shakespeare Stout, and Lind Brewing's Sir Francis Stout, not to mention specialty stouts like Anderson Valley Oatmeal Stout and the unique Alaskan Smoked Porter.

In general, stout implies more body and flavor than porter, but there is considerable overlap. Both styles tend to have rich malt flavors on the palate, often with coffee and chocolate notes, and moderate to high hop bitterness; they may finish dry or slightly sweet.

For all their strength, these beers can go with strikingly delicate foods like raw oysters. I also like a good porter or dry stout with roast beef or Chicken with Mushroom Cream Sauce (variation, page 42), where the dry and hoppy finish cleanses the palate for the next bite.

Petites Gougères

■ *Makes 18*

A gougère is a traditional Burgundian savory pastry made with Swiss-style cheese, baked in a large ring shape. Individual puffs are easier both to bake and to serve.

1 cup milk, whole or reduced-fat

4 tablespoons unsalted butter

½ teaspoon kosher salt

Pinch of freshly ground white pepper

1 cup all-purpose flour

4 or 5 eggs, at room temperature

3 ounces French or Swiss Gruyère cheese, diced into ¼-inch pieces

Milk, for brushing

WHICH BEER?

Try these as an appetizer with a hoppy pale ale.

Preheat the oven to 400°F. Lightly grease 2 baking sheets. Combine the milk, butter, salt, and pepper in a heavy-bottomed saucepan and bring to a boil. Remove the pan from the heat and add the flour all at once. Stir vigorously with a wooden spoon until the liquid absorbs the flour. Return the pan to low heat and cook, stirring constantly, until the mixture pulls away from the sides of the pan.

Transfer the dough to a bowl, leaving behind any that sticks to the pan. Let cool 5 minutes. (This is a good time to dice the cheese if you haven't already done so.) Add the eggs, one at a time, beating the dough until each egg is thoroughly incorporated before adding the next. Four eggs should be enough to make a moist, glossy dough; if not, work in the fifth egg.

Stir the cheese cubes into the dough. Drop by heaping tablespoonfuls onto the baking sheets, or use a pastry bag with a plain tip to make 2-inch domes. Smooth the tops with a brush dipped in milk. Bake until the puffs are golden brown and sound hollow when tapped, 25 to 35 minutes. Serve warm or at room temperature.

TECHNIQUE NOTE Congratulations! You have just learned to make *pâte à choux*, the classic French dough used for cream puffs and éclairs.

Based on trials with other cheeses, including cheddar types and aged Asiago, I think it's best to stick with Gruyère and other dense Swiss types; other cheeses seem to melt too fast, running out before the puffs are set.

A Note About Salt

■

All of the recipes in this book were developed with kosher salt, specifically the Diamond Crystal brand in the red box, because I prefer its flavor to that of the typical granulated table salt sold in cylindrical boxes. If you use granulated salt, bear in mind that teaspoon for teaspoon, cup for cup, it contains twice as much salt as kosher salt—not because of the differences in chemical makeup, but because of the large, flaky shape of the kosher salt crystals. There's simply more empty space in a spoonful of the latter than the former. (Try it for yourself if you have an accurate scale; weigh an equal volume of each, say $1/4$ to $1/3$ cup.) If you use granulated salt in recipes that call for measured amounts, start with half as much as is called for in the recipe and adjust to taste.

I have never found sea salt to be worth the extra cost, but if you use it, you will need to figure out the ratio for the brand you use.

Whisky-Cured Salmon with Whole-Grain Mustard Sauce

■ *Serves 8-10*

This falls somewhere between Scandinavian-style gravlax and a cheater's form of smoked salmon. A lot of gravlax variations call for aquavit, gin, or other spirits; here a splash of single-malt Scotch adds a faint smoky touch, which you can reinforce with a little liquid smoke. With or without the added smoke, it makes a delicately flavored and textured salmon appetizer to go on thin slices of bread, either whole slices of the little loaves labeled "party rye" or larger slices cut into triangles. Leftovers are also good on bagels.

I'm not a big fan of farm-raised salmon, but I prefer it here for safety reasons (see the note at the end of the end of the recipe). I find that serving farmed salmon raw turns its biggest drawback—its high fat content—into a virtue.

1 pound farm-raised king or Atlantic salmon fillet (see Note), in one piece with skin on, pin bones removed

$1/8$ teaspoon liquid smoke (optional)

1 tablespoon single-malt Scotch whisky

3 tablespoons kosher salt

3 tablespoons brown sugar

$1/2$ teaspoon freshly ground white pepper

SAUCE

2 tablespoons whole-grain-style prepared mustard

2 tablespoons mild olive oil or neutral vegetable oil

$1/2$ teaspoon sugar, or to taste

■

Thinly sliced rye or pumpernickel bread

WHICH BEER?

Try this with your favorite hefeweizen; I also like it with a berry-flavored wheat beer like Widmer Widberry.

Rinse the fish and pat dry. Place the fillet skin side down in a glass or stainless dish. If using the liquid smoke, combine it with the whisky in a small bowl, and brush or rub the mixture on the fish; if using straight whisky, sprinkle it on straight from the bottle and brush or rub it all over the fish. Let stand 30 minutes uncovered in the refrigerator.

Combine the salt, sugar, and pepper and spread the mixture evenly all over the fish, a bit heavier where the meat is thickest. Cover loosely with plastic wrap and set another pan (such as a loaf pan) on top. Add 2 to 3 pounds of weight inside the second pan (a quart jar of mayonnaise, a bottle of wine, whatever). Place in the refrigerator, with a prop under one end to tilt it slightly. Let cure 2 to 3 days, then brush off any remaining salt crystals. Wrap tightly and keep in the refrigerator up to 5 days.

Whisk together the sauce ingredients and adjust the sugar to taste, bearing in mind the sweetness and saltiness of the salmon cure.

To serve, slice the salmon thinly on the diagonal, across rather than parallel to the layers of muscle. Serve on the bread slices, topped with a dollop of sauce.

NOTE While I prefer wild salmon whenever possible, for this kind of raw preparation it's safer to use a farm-raised fish. With their processed feed, farmed salmon are never exposed to the parasites found in the marine food chain. One of these, a tiny worm called *Anisakis simplex*, is common in West Coast waters and may be found in wild salmon. Cold curing, cold smoking, and similar preparations do not kill the worms, so eating gravlax made with local wild salmon creates some risk of ingesting live parasites. While human *Anisakis* infection is very rare, and serious complications are rarer still, even this low level of risk is avoidable. That being said, lots of people enjoy wild salmon cured in these ways. The choice is up to you.

Mussels Steamed in Wheat Beer

■ *Serves 2 as an appetizer*

The trickiest thing about steaming mussels or clams in beer is finding the right beer, assuming that you want to slurp up the broth along with the shellfish. Again, it's the old hops problem: Boil down a hoppy beer and you concentrate its bitterness. The Belgians, among the world's most enthusiastic mussel eaters, figured this out a long time ago, and the favorite beer there for steaming mussels is a sour-tasting lambic, which is made with hops that have been aged to reduce their bitterness. I have yet to taste a domestic beer that comes close to the flavor profile of lambic, but a lightly hopped domestic hefeweizen or a wheat beer in the "wit" style works pretty well.

Even if you like lemon in your wheat beers, don't assume that this dish will be improved by a squeeze of lemon in the bowl. I've tried it both ways and prefer it without lemon.

1 pound live mussels

½ cup wheat beer

1 tablespoon chopped shallot or green onion

1 teaspoon minced parsley or chervil

Pinch of freshly ground black pepper

1 or 2 tablespoons butter (optional)

Lemon wedges (optional)

WHICH BEER?
Clearly, the same beer you cook
the mussels in.

Scrub and debeard the mussels, discarding any open ones that do not close when handled. Place in a skillet or saucepan with the beer, shallot, parsley, pepper, and butter. Cover, bring to a boil, and steam until the shells are all open. Serve in bowls, with a soup spoon and bread for dipping in the broth. (A separate bowl for the empty shells is a nice touch.) Squeeze a little lemon juice into the broth in your bowl if you like, but taste it first!

Oysters on the Half Shell

■ *Serves as many as you like*

To those who love them, there is little that can compare with a cold, plump, raw oyster, sipped from its shell with its tiny bit of retained seawater. Served with a squeeze of lemon or a bit of tangy sauce, it's the perfect thing to go with a surprising range of beers. I include them in this chapter because oysters go marvelously with a dry Irish-style stout.

To my taste, a perfectly balanced oyster needs no sauce or other adornment, but most people like to season oysters with something acid, such as a squeeze of lemon or a bit of Mignonette Sauce (recipe follows). Either one adds a refreshing touch of acidity that goes well with the richness of almost any oyster, and can be just the thing to bring a bland or fatty oyster into balance. I've also included a salsa-type topping based on tomatillos and a très chic frozen tomato sauce.

Oysters (3 or 4 to a dozen per person, depending on your appetite and budget)

Lemon wedges

Mignonette Sauce, Tomatillo Salsa Cruda, or Tomato Granita (recipes follow)

Hold an oyster with the deeper side of the oyster down in your well-protected palm (see page 26); or if you prefer, lay the oyster on the table with a hand on top. Find the hinge point of the shell. With whatever combination of swiveling and wiggling gets the job done, gently work the tip of the knife between the shell halves until you feel you have some leverage (¼ inch or so is plenty of penetration; any deeper and you risk cutting up the meat inside). Twist (do not push) the knife and pry upward to pop the shell open.

When you have popped the hinge, slide the knife in along the top shell to cut it free from the central adductor muscle. Discard the top shell. Now slide the knife under the oyster to cut the other end of the muscle free from the bottom valve. Finally, remove any bits of grit, mud, or broken shell, rearrange the edges of the oyster if they have been disturbed, and the oyster is ready to serve, with a squeeze of lemon or your choice of sauces.

WHICH BEER?

I would go to either extreme here—a dry stout or a delicate hefeweizen. With stout, I love the way the oyster and beer flavors circle around each other long after you have swallowed the oyster. Hefeweizen acts more like the traditional dry white wine, cleansing and refreshing the palate and setting it up for another oyster and another sip.

Mignonette Sauce
■

1 tablespoon minced shallot

1 tablespoon sherry vinegar or other wine vinegar

Freshly ground black pepper

Combine the shallot and vinegar, and season to taste with pepper. If the mixture seems too tart, cut it with a tiny bit of water. A quarter to a half teaspoon of the mixture is about right for spooning on top of each oyster.

Tomatillo Salsa Cruda
■

6 small fresh tomatillos

1 small green onion, minced

$1/2$ serrano chile, seeds and ribs removed, minced

Kosher salt

Peel and halve the tomatillos (see page 158) and grate the cut sides on a box grater. Add the green onion and serrano chile to the tomatillo. Salt to taste and chill thoroughly before serving.

Tomato Granita
■

1 small ripe tomato, peeled, seeded, and finely chopped

1 teaspoon minced shallot

$1/2$ teaspoon white wine vinegar

Pinch of kosher salt

Combine the tomato, shallot, vinegar, and salt. Place in a small bowl or plastic container and freeze, removing it from the freezer every 20 minutes or so to stir and break up the ice crystals. Use a small melon scoop or spoon to scrape out about $1/2$ teaspoon granita per oyster.

Oyster Basics

■

If you already know how to buy and shuck oysters, you can skip most of the following.

First, choose smallish oysters intended for serving on the half shell, not the enormous ones sold in Chinese markets. West Coast oyster growers provide us with dozens of site-named Pacific or Miyagi oysters, as well as their smaller cousins the Kumamoto oyster, the native Olympia, and the European flat or Belon type. The East Coast oyster most widely available in the West is the Malpeque from eastern Canada, but you may find others from up and down the Atlantic Coast. Each has a slightly different flavor, and they change from month to month, making this a fascinating ongoing study. Your best bet is to find a fish market you trust (preferably with a changing selection) and go with what they recommend.

Oysters need to be kept alive until shucking, which means keeping them cold and moist. They should be displayed on ice in the market, with the deeper shell halves downward. When you get home, unpack them, scrub off any grit from the shells with a brush, and lay them right side up in a bowl. Cover them with a damp towel, and refrigerate until ready to shuck. Don't store oysters in water or they will die. Reject at the market any open oysters that do not close when handled, and discard any that die after that.

If you shuck oysters regularly, invest in a proper oyster knife, with a thick, blunt-edged blade that is strong enough to pry the shells apart without breaking. Otherwise, you can get by with the combination of a "church key" can opener or a small, clean screwdriver for the prying part of the job and a paring knife for the cutting part. To protect your other hand, either wear a heavy protective glove or cradle the oyster in several thicknesses of folded kitchen towel.

Curried Beef Pasties

■ *Makes eight 6-inch pies*

Cornish pasties (pronounced long "a", the "r" somehow having been dropped from "pastry") are turnover-shaped meat pies originally baked for Cornish miners to take into the mines for lunch. One theory holds that the thick rolled edge of the crust served as a disposable handle, so a miner could eat the rest of the pie without worrying about toxic stuff on his hands.

These are smaller pasties, and you can definitely eat the whole crust. I was struggling to come up with just the right dough texture—some of the flakiness of a good pie dough but a little less rich, and strong enough for the pie to be picked up without shattering the crust—when my wife said, "Sounds like knishes." She pulled out her grandmother's knish recipe from a card file, I tried it, and bingo! So just imagine you're a Russian-Jewish grandmother running a bakery in Cornwall. . . .

FILLING

1 large russet potato (8 to 10 ounces)

²/₃ pound ground beef

1¹/₂ cups minced onion (1 large)

Heaping teaspoon curry powder

Kosher salt and freshly ground black pepper

DOUGH

1¹/₂ cups flour

¹/₂ teaspoon kosher salt

2 tablespoons cold butter

1 tablespoon cold vegetable shortening, lard,
  or rendered chicken fat (see Note)

1 egg, beaten

About 3 tablespoons cold water

■

¹/₄ cup milk, for brushing

WHICH BEER?

Your favorite ale, as bitter or as mild as you like. The little bit of curry powder here isn't going to quarrel with any beer's flavor.

Boil the potato in its skin just until tender. Meanwhile, cook the meat in a skillet over low heat until the raw color is gone and the meat begins to brown. Remove the meat from the skillet with a slotted spoon and swab out most of the fat with a paper towel. Add the onion and cook until translucent. Add the curry powder and return the beef to the skillet. Peel the cooked potato, dice finely, and add it to the skillet. Cook for a few minutes, moistening with a little of the potato water if it is in danger of scorching. Season to taste with salt and pepper (it should be highly seasoned, as the dough is on the bland side) and let cool.

For the dough, combine the flour, salt, and fats in a bowl and cut the fat into small pieces. Rub the mixture between your fingertips, breaking up the lumps of fat into small flakes. Stir in the egg (leave a tiny bit behind in the bowl for brushing), then add cold water, a tablespoon at a time, stirring with the fingers of one hand, until the dough just comes together. Shape into a ball, wrap tightly, and refrigerate 30 minutes to overnight.

Preheat the oven to 375°F. Divide the dough into 6 equal-size pieces (a scale is handy for this). On a lightly floured surface, roll a piece of dough into a 7-inch circle and spoon ⅓ cup of the filling on one side. Fold the dough over, press the edges together, and then fold about ½ inch of the edge up and inward in a series of pleats. Transfer to a baking sheet. Repeat with the remaining dough and filling. Stir the milk into the egg remaining in the bowl, brush the tops of the pies with a little of this mixture, and make a couple of slits in the tops. Bake until golden brown, about 25 minutes. Serve warm.

NOTE You can make this crust with all butter if you like, or a variety of other fats. Lard is a traditional fat for savory pies in England, and before Crisco, Jewish immigrants from Eastern Europe used chicken fat rendered with onions for flavor. Shortening gives a nice, flaky crust but no flavor, and the more we learn about the trans fatty acids in hydrogenated vegetable oils, the less I want to use them. My preferred blend is equal parts unsalted butter and chicken fat.

VARIATION For Sausage Pasties, substitute bulk pork sausage for the ground beef and omit the curry powder.

Pork Loin Stuffed with Prunes

■ *Serves 4 to 6*

Pork has changed so much in recent decades that cooking times and temper-atures in most older recipes should be suspect. The earlier practice of cooking pork until no trace of pink remains (an internal temperature of 175°F or more) was based on a fear of trichinosis, a parasitic disease, and also on much fattier animals.

Today, trichinosis has been virtually eradicated from commercial pork (and any lingering risk is eliminated by cooking to a mere 140°F). More important, today's pork is much leaner than that of a generation ago, and thus less forgiving of overcooking. If you can get over old prejudices, you will find it most flavorful and juicy at the medium stage, when the meat is still slightly pink and the juices definitely run pink. For further insurance against drying, I always brine lean cuts of pork like the loin (see "Brining for Flavor and Moisture," page 208).

One thing that has not changed is pork's affinity for fruit flavors and sweet and tart mixtures. Prunes are a traditional Middle European stuffing ingredi-ent; dried apricots (plumped in water if especially dry) also work well. Sweet and Sour Red Cabbage (recipe follows) makes a perfect accompaniment.

BRINE

4 cups water

3 tablespoons kosher salt

1 tablespoon brown sugar

1 bay leaf

$1/2$ teaspoon peppercorns

$1/2$ teaspoon fennel seed

■

1 boneless pork loin roast, $1^1/2$ to 2 pounds, trimmed of any excess fat

Scant cup (about 4 ounces) pitted prunes

$1/2$ cup warm unsalted chicken or vegetable stock

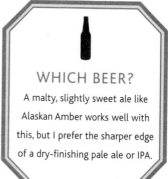

WHICH BEER?
A malty, slightly sweet ale like Alaskan Amber works well with this, but I prefer the sharper edge of a dry-finishing pale ale or IPA.

Combine the brine ingredients in a large bowl or 4-cup measure, stirring to dissolve the salt. Place the meat in a strong, food-grade plastic bag (a gallon-size sealable bag is ideal), pour in the brine, and gather up the bag to surround the meat and expel all the air. Seal the bag and refrigerate 6 hours to overnight. Drain, rinse, and pat dry before roasting.

Insert the tip of a boning knife into the center of the roast from one end and cut a slit about an inch wide. Make a matching slit from the other end. Insert a straight, slender tool (a clean sharpening steel works best, or the handle of a wooden spoon) into the slit and force it through, making one continuous tunnel the length of the roast. Stuff prunes into the tunnel from both ends. If the roast is in danger of coming apart, tie it in 3 or 4 places with cotton twine. (The roast can be prepared to this point several hours before roasting and refrigerated; if time permits, remove it from the refrigerator a good 30 minutes before roasting.)

Preheat the oven to 400°F. Place the roast fat side up in a roasting pan and roast to an internal temperature of 145°F, about 45 minutes. Remove from the pan and let rest on a platter, loosely covered, while you deglaze the roasting pan as follows. The internal temperature will rise by 5° to 10° as the roast rests.

Swab out the fat from the roasting pan with a paper towel. Pour in the stock and scrape the pan well to dissolve the browned drippings. Strain the sauce into a warmed bowl, let it settle for a few minutes, and skim the fat off the surface with a ladle.

Slice the roast crosswise and arrange the slices on a warm platter. Drizzle with a little of the pan sauce and pass the remaining sauce on the side.

Sweet and Sour Red Cabbage

■ *Serves 6*

You can vary this dish by changing the fat. Bacon fat or pancetta is always delicious; so is chicken fat, either rendered with onion in the Jewish style or simply taken off the top of chilled chicken stock. Or use duck fat from Duck Confit (page 75). If you are making this to go with a pork roast, you can simply render out a little of the fat trimmed from the roast while you slice the cabbage and onions.

1 tablespoon fat (from chicken, bacon, duck, or fresh pork) or mild
    vegetable oil

1 pound red cabbage (about half a typical head), cored and thinly
    sliced

1 medium onion, thinly sliced

¾ teaspoon kosher salt

Freshly ground black pepper

2 tablespoons cider vinegar

1 tablespoon brown sugar or honey, or to taste

Melt the fat in a deep, flameproof casserole over medium heat. Add the
remaining ingredients and cook, stirring to distribute the seasonings,
until the cabbage begins to soften. Cover and simmer over low heat
until tender but not mushy, 1½ to 2 hours. Adjust the seasonings to
taste.

Carbonnade of Beef Braised in Beer

■ *Serves 6*

Probably the most famous dish cooked with beer is carbonnade flamande, beef slices stewed Flemish style in beer with an ample amount of sliced onions made sweet by slow braising. Just as coq au vin can be cooked with whatever wine is at hand, carbonnade can in theory be made in many different "flavors" by varying the beer. In northern France near the Belgian border, the beer is mainly reddish, fruity ale. At least one authentic Flemish version would be made with one of that region's tart-flavored wheat beers, such as lambic or gueuze. In search of a West Coast version of this dish (carbonnade cascadienne?), I have made this dish with various West Coast beers, from hefeweizen (which makes a tasty but rather pale stew, especially with a little extra vinegar) to a brown ale like Lost Coast Downtown Brown (my favorite for both flavor and deep brown color) to porter and stout. Feel free to experiment, but watch out for highly hopped ales, or the stew can come out too bitter.

Serve with egg noodles or roasted new potatoes.

1 beef rump roast, 2 to 2¹⁄₂ pounds

Kosher salt and freshly ground black pepper

4 tablespoons oil

2 pounds onions, thinly sliced

2 tablespoons flour

2 cups unsalted beef, veal, or poultry stock, or low-sodium canned beef broth

12 ounces not very bitter ale

1 tablespoon wine or cider vinegar

1 bay leaf

1 sprig fresh thyme, or ¹⁄₄ teaspoon dried thyme

Sugar to taste, if needed

WHICH BEER?

It's hard to go wrong serving the same beer you cook with, but you can also serve something with more hop bitterness than would be good in the dish.

Preheat the oven to 250°F. Trim as much fat as possible from the roast and slice the meat across the grain into ¼-inch slices. Season the slices well with salt and pepper (go easy on the salt if using canned broth). Heat 1 tablespoon of the oil in a skillet over medium-high heat and sear the meat, a few slices at a time, until nicely browned on both sides. Transfer to a plate as they are done.

Reduce the heat to medium-low; if the meat has released a lot of liquid, let it cook until the skillet is nearly dry but not in danger of scorching. Add the remaining 3 tablespoons oil and the onions and cook, stirring and turning with a long fork, until the onions are soft and lightly browned, about 10 minutes. Push the onions to one side of the pan and stir in the flour. Cook, stirring and scraping the pan, until the flour mixture (roux) turns a medium brown; keep an eye on the onions so they do not burn. Add the stock, ale, vinegar, and accumulated juices from the meat plate to the pan and stir everything together. Bring to a simmer, cook until any lumps of roux are dissolved, and season to taste.

Spoon a little of the sauce mixture into the bottom of a covered baking dish. Arrange the beef slices in the dish, then top with the onions and sauce, bay leaf, and thyme. Cover and bake 2 hours. Taste the sauce for balance, and add a little sugar if the sauce is on the bitter side. If the meat is not yet fork-tender, continue baking for another ½ hour or so.

Let the stew stand for a few minutes out of the oven, then skim off any excess fat around the edges. Or refrigerate it for up to several days and remove any hardened fat before reheating in a low oven.

TECHNIQUE NOTE The instructions here call for a heavy skillet for the stovetop cooking steps and another covered casserole dish for slow cooking in the oven. If you have a suitable covered pan that can go straight from the stovetop to the oven (an enameled cast-iron Dutch oven, a deep, stainless-lined sauté pan, or some type of flameproof earthenware), you can do everything in that one pan, nestling the browned beef slices into the sauce and onion mixture before baking.

Choucroute Garni des Brasseurs
(Sauerkraut Braised with Assorted Meats)

■ *Serves 4*

Wine-drinking France and beer-drinking France meet in Alsace, the north-eastern region bordering the Rhine. In its classical form, choucroute garni is made to harmonize with the dry, flavorful white wines of the region, requiring extensive rinsing and draining of the sauerkraut to minimize its sour, briny flavors. Well, beer has no problem going with the full-strength taste of sauer-kraut, so I give the sauerkraut only a quick draining before cooking it with the meats and seasonings. This is how I imagine brewers rather than winemakers would enjoy their choucroute.

This recipe is easy to scale up for a crowd, and it is still good when barely warm, making it a good choice for a weekend open house or a crowd gath-ered for a ball game on TV.

2 cups sauerkraut

1 tablespoon oil, poultry fat, or bacon drippings

1 cup thinly sliced onion

1 teaspoon dill seed

2 bay leaves

1 teaspoon juniper berries, or a splash of gin

$1/3$ cup water

$1/2$ pound cooked ham, in large cubes, or
  smoked pork chops

1 to $1/2$ pounds fully cooked garlic sausages

Set the sauerkraut in a colander to drain; rinse it lightly if you like the dish less krauty. Heat the oil in a Dutch oven and cook the onion until soft. Add the drained sauerkraut, dill seed, bay leaves, juniper berries, and water and place the ham on top. Cover and cook over low heat 30 minutes, or longer if you like the sauerkraut more tender; add a little more water if it is in danger of cooking dry.

Puncture the sausages and add them to the pot. Cook until plump and heated through, 10 to 15 minutes. Remove the bay leaves before serving. Serve with good rye bread and mustard.

VARIATION For the garlic sausage, substitute other fine-textured, fully cooked sausages like bockwurst/weisswurst (two names for very similar "white" sausages), knockwurst, or bratwurst. For a buffet dish, use an assortment of sausages, cut into 2-inch chunks.

A smoked ham shank gives a nice flavor and body to the dish but needs longer cooking. Have the butcher cut the shank crosswise in 2 or 3 places, and plan on at least an hour for the shank and sauerkraut to cook together. Don't worry about overcooking—in France they cook this dish for 3 hours or more.

WHICH BEER?

I like the crispness of a Pilsner-style lager with this, or maybe a Märzen, but nothing much heavier than that.

Classic Standing Rib Roast

■ *Serves 6 to 8 (8 to 10)*

So you owe two other couples a dinner. Assuming they all eat meat, there's nothing simpler yet more impressive than a big hunk of roast beef. And if you're going to serve roast beef, you might as well go all the way and serve a standing rib roast. Go to the best butcher shop in town, the one that sells Certified Angus or other USDA Choice beef, and plan to drop a couple of twenties just for the meat. It will still work out cheaper than taking all those folks out for a "prime rib" dinner. Your beer budget will also go a lot farther at retail than at restaurant prices.

Butcher terminology varies, but for the least waste and the easiest carving, ask for a small end rib-eye roast with bones. This is the most severely trimmed version of rib roast, basically the "eye" or main rib muscle with a minimum layer of fat and just the rib bones (no backbone or "chine") attached. You get the flavor and moisture benefits of a roast cooked with the bones, but very little waste.

Among my family and friends, a two-bone rib-eye roast weighing about 4 pounds, the smallest you are likely to find, will feed six amply and eight modestly. If you know you are cooking for big appetites, bite the bullet and get a three-bone roast, which will provide lots of leftover roast beef for sandwiches, even after serving eight to ten. The meaty ribs can be reheated with your favorite barbecue sauce to serve one or two. The quantities given here are for a two-bone roast, with the three-bone amounts in parentheses.

WHICH BEER?

Porter, stout, or pale ale.

2 (3) teaspoons kosher salt

Scant (heaping) teaspoon coarsely cracked black pepper

2 small (large) cloves garlic, minced

1 two- or three-bone rib roast with bones, preferably USDA Choice, 4 to 7 pounds

1½ (2) pounds small new potatoes

½ (¾) cup hot unsalted chicken, beef, or veal stock, or water

Individual Spinach Soufflés (recipe follows)

Combine the salt, pepper, and garlic and rub the mixture all over the roast. Place bone side down in a roasting pan large enough to hold the roast and the potatoes, and set aside for 30 minutes to 2 hours at room temperature.

Preheat the oven to 500°F. Scatter the potatoes in the roasting pan. Add the roast, place in the oven, roast 15 minutes, and then (without opening the oven door) reduce the oven heat to 325°F. Reset the timer for 15 minutes per pound for a roast that is rare in the center. Meanwhile, prepare the base for the Individual Spinach Soufflés.

When the timer goes off, check the roast with an instant-read thermometer; you are looking for an internal temperature of 120°F for a medium-rare roast, 115°F for rare. (It will go higher as it sits out of the oven.) When the roast reaches the desired temperature, remove it from the oven and set it aside, loosely covered with foil. Reset the oven to 375°F and proceed with the soufflés.

When the soufflés are in the oven, transfer the roast to a carving board with a channel to catch the juices (or, lacking that, a smallish board set in a rimmed sheet pan). Transfer the potatoes to a serving dish. Pour out the clear fat from a corner of the roasting pan, keeping any dark brown juices that settle to the bottom. Add the stock to the pan and scrape up the browned bits from the bottom. If your roasting pan is flameproof, heat it on top of the stove while you deglaze it; otherwise, scrape the contents into a small saucepan and simmer until reduced slightly.

To carve the roast in the classic manner, stand it up on one end and hold it steady with a fork while you slice horizontally to the bone, then slide the knife along the bone to free the slice. A less classical but somewhat easier technique is to set the roast on the cutting board in the same position in which it roasted, then tip it up on its large side to expose the bones; carve down along the bones to free the whole rib eye from the bones, then lay the roast back down and slice the meat crosswise. Offer the first slice to the guest who likes meat closer to medium.

Individual Spinach Soufflés

■ *Serves 8*

This recipe combines and replaces two classic accompaniments to roast beef, creamed spinach and Yorkshire pudding. You will need as many ramekins (the kind that look like miniature soufflé dishes, about 3½ inches across and half as deep) as you have guests; otherwise, see the variation below.

The timing assumes that you are making these to go with the roast on page 36, and baking them while the roast rests before carving. You can cook the spinach and make the sauce anytime while the meat is in the oven, or up to an hour ahead, but don't start beating the egg whites until the oven is available. If you've never made a soufflé before, you'd better start with the standard whole form in the variation following the recipe.

Leaves and tender stems from 1 bunch spinach

3 tablespoons butter

3 tablespoons flour

1 cup milk

Scant teaspoon kosher salt

Pinch of freshly ground white pepper or cayenne

⅛ teaspoon ground nutmeg

¼ cup grated Parmesan

5 eggs, at room temperature

Preheat (or reset) the oven to 375°F.

Wash the spinach in several changes of water until no dirt remains. Lift the leaves out of the water into a saucepan, then drain off as much water as you can from the pan. Cover and cook over low heat, turning occasionally, until all the spinach has wilted. Uncover and let sit until cool enough to handle, then squeeze out as much liquid as possible. Chop the spinach finely and set aside. (If you're bothered by throwing away all the vitamins in the "pot liquor" from cooking the spinach, then pour it into a glass and drink it. It's good for you, and the taste isn't half bad.)

Melt 2½ tablespoons of the butter in a medium saucepan and stir in the flour. Cook this mixture (roux) over medium-low heat until the flour just begins to color, 3 to 5 minutes. Transfer the roux to a heat-proof container (a metal measuring cup works fine), then add the milk to the empty saucepan and bring to a simmer. Add the roux back to the hot milk and stir with a whisk to dissolve any lumps as the sauce thickens. Season the sauce with salt, pepper, and nutmeg, stir in the chopped spinach and half the cheese, and adjust the seasoning. Set aside until ready to add the eggs. Rub the inside of eight 4-ounce ramekins with the remaining ½ tablespoon butter, dust the insides with Parmesan, and turn to coat the bottom and sides with the cheese before knocking out the excess.

Separate the eggs, dropping the whites into a mixing bowl and adding 4 of the yolks to the spinach mixture (save the remaining yolk for another purpose, or discard it). Stir the sauce to incorporate the yolks. Beat the egg whites with a wire whisk or an egg beater to the stiff peak stage (when you invert the beater, the egg white that drips off will hold its shape rather than flopping over). Immediately scoop a quarter of the beaten whites into the sauce, using a rubber spatula, and stir gently to combine, then fold this mixture into the bowl of whites until combined (see the Technique Note). Scoop and pour the mixture into the prepared ramekins, distributing the sauce and whites as evenly as possible, and dust the tops with any remaining cheese. Set the ramekins in a sheet pan or roasting pan (for easier handling) and place immediately in the middle of the preheated oven. Bake until a knife inserted in the center comes out clean, 15 to 18 minutes (do not open the oven during the first 12 minutes or the soufflés may fall). Set the ramekins directly on the dinner plates and serve immediately.

TECHNIQUE NOTE To "fold" ingredients into egg whites, whipped cream, or other light mixtures, insert a rubber spatula vertically into the center of the bowl, push it to the bottom, then scoop it toward the side of the bowl and upward, lifting some of the mixture and finally turning it out onto the top. Give the bowl a quarter turn and repeat the process until the mixture is fairly even. The idea is to combine the lighter and heavier elements without knocking all the air out of the lighter one.

VARIATION If you don't have enough ramekins to make individual soufflés, you can get pretty good results making a dozen in an ordinary muffin pan; use a knife and narrow spatula to remove them in the latter case, and figure that some of them will get mangled. (If they don't, some folks get seconds.) It's probably better just to make a normal soufflé in an 8-cup baking dish and scoop out servings at the table. Cooking time for an 8-cup soufflé will be more like 25 minutes at 375°F.

Sautéed Chicken Breasts with Mushroom Sauce

■ *Serves 4*

Very simple, but very good, this dish should be in every cook's repertoire. The toast is optional, but I like the way it soaks up the excess sauce. You can use ordinary button mushrooms or fancy varieties like chanterelles, hedgehogs, morels, or fresh shiitake (I don't like the last, but I know a lot of people do). When you want to throw calorie caution to the wind, make the variation with cream that follows the recipe. In either case, serve with a bright green vegetable like sugar snap peas.

2 cups unsalted chicken stock

4 chicken breast halves, boned and skinned

Kosher salt and freshly ground black pepper

Flour, for dredging

2 to 3 tablespoons olive oil

1 tablespoon minced shallot, or ¼ cup minced green onion

¾ pound mushrooms (button, oyster, chanterelle, or an assortment), sliced ¼ inch thick

3 tablespoons dry sherry or Madeira

Dash of sweet soy sauce (see Note)

4 slices bread, crusts removed, toasted and lightly buttered (optional)

1 tablespoon chopped chives, for garnish (omit if using green onion)

WHICH BEER?

Just about any beer; I especially like a dry-finishing porter with the cream version. Alaskan Smoked Porter is an intriguing variation on the theme.

Bring the stock to a boil, reduce the heat to a lively simmer, and cook until the volume is reduced to about ½ cup. (This can be done ahead of time.)

Have a warm serving dish or individual warm plates ready. Season the chicken breasts lightly with salt and pepper. Spread some flour on a dinner plate. Heat a 10- or 12-inch skillet over medium-high heat with enough of the oil to lightly cover the bottom. Dredge a chicken breast in the flour, shake off the excess, and add to the pan smooth side down. Repeat with the remaining breasts. Cook until nicely browned on the first side, turn, and brown on the other side. Transfer to the serving dish as soon as the thickest part feels springy.

Add a bit more oil if the skillet seems dry. Add the shallots, cook for a few seconds, and add the mushrooms. Cook until the mushrooms exude their liquid, then add the sherry and soy sauce and cook until the liquid is nearly gone. Add the reduced stock, bring to a boil, taste for seasoning, and adjust if necessary. Return the chicken breasts to the pan, along with any juices that have accumulated on the plate, reheat briefly, and arrange the breasts on the platter or on top of the optional toasts. Spoon the sauce over the top and serve immediately, garnished with chives.

NOTE A little soy sauce and a touch of sweetness do wonders for mushroom flavor, even outside of an Asian context. If you have a sweet, thick Southeast Asian soy sauce such as the Thai *kwong hung seng* or Indonesian *kecap manis* on hand, it is ideal for this recipe. I wouldn't go out and buy some just for this purpose (ordinary soy sauce will do, plus a pinch of sugar if the sauce needs more rounding), but look for some the next time you are shopping in an Asian market.

VARIATION

Chicken Breasts with Mushroom Cream Sauce

Use only 1 cup stock and add $^2/_3$ cup whipping cream or crème fraîche (see Note, page 185) to the stock before boiling. Bring to a boil and reduce by about a third.

Medallions of Venison with Currant Sauce

■ *Serves 4*

A lot of traditional game recipes use fruit sauces to balance (some would say mask) strong gamy flavor in the meat. Today, almost all venison commercially available in this country comes not from hunters but from deer raised on farms (a lot of it in New Zealand). Although the flavor is milder than that of wild venison, it's still a very flavorful, deep-colored meat that goes well with a touch of fruit in the sauce.

Roe deer (the favorite species of farmers) falls somewhere between lamb and pork in size, so the strip loin, the cut that yields a New York steak in beef and the larger half of center-cut pork chops, measures about 1½ by 3 inches in cross section. Two little steaks or "medallions" cut from the strip loin make a restaurant-style portion of 4 to 5 ounces, which, given the rich flavor of the meat and the sauce (not to mention the steep price), is plenty.

Serve with Garlic Mashed Potatoes (page 209), plain mashed potatoes, or Wild Mushroom Risotto (page 85), and boiled or steamed sugar snap peas or cut green beans.

2½ cups unsalted veal, beef, or poultry stock

²⁄₃ cup dry red wine (preferably a not too tannic syrah, zinfandel, or Rhône red)

1 pound boneless venison strip loin, cut crosswise into ¾-inch medallions

1 tablespoon olive or grapeseed oil

Kosher salt and freshly ground black pepper

Heaping tablespoon minced shallot

2 teaspoons red currant jelly

2 tablespoons butter

WHICH BEER?
This is good with pale ale or porter, but it's even better with a Belgian-style "abbey" ale, the red Burgundy of the beer world.

Combine the stock and wine in a small saucepan and bring to a boil. Turn down the heat to a lively simmer and reduce the volume of the liquid by two thirds. (An easy way to do this is to measure the depth before you start with a wooden spoon or spatula, and use this as a "dipstick" to check the volume as it reduces.)

Remove the meat from the refrigerator 30 minutes before cooking. Put 4 dinner plates in a very low oven to warm.

Heat a nonstick skillet over medium-high heat and add a film of oil. Season the medallions with a little salt and pepper and blot away any juices. Add to the pan and cook until nicely browned on the first side, about 3 minutes. Turn and continue cooking until the meat is rare to medium rare (see the Technique Note), another 2 to 3 minutes. Divide among the dinner plates. Add the shallots to the skillet and cook until they begin to soften. Add the reduced stock and wine and the currant jelly, bring to a boil, and cook until reduced by half. Meanwhile, put a mound of potatoes or risotto in the middle of each plate next to the medallions. Taste the sauce and adjust the seasoning. Add the butter and stir or swirl the pan until the butter melts. Spoon the sauce over and around the medallions and garnish with peas or green beans.

TECHNIQUE NOTE As rich as it tastes, venison is lean meat, so don't overcook it (and anything past medium rare, possibly medium, is overcooked to my taste). If you are comfortable with a fingertip test to tell how beef is cooked—feeling the difference between the flabbiness of raw meat and the increasing degrees of springiness as it cooks through rare and medium-rare to medium—you can apply the same test to venison medallions. If not, you might want to practice on beef a few times before shelling out for venison.

Cod Baked in Cider

■ *Serves 4*

Cod and its relatives hake and whiting are frequently cooked and served with dry hard cider in the "cider belt" of northwest Europe, from the Celtic northern coast of Spain through Brittany to England and Ireland. Until the West Coast microbrew industry gives us a really dry cider, try this with the driest one you can find (see page 46).

If you have a shallow flameproof casserole that can go from the stovetop to the oven to the table, it's ideal for this dish. Otherwise, start it in a skillet and finish in a baking dish.

3 tablespoons mild oil

2 large white new potatoes, scrubbed and diced

1 large onion, thinly sliced

$^1/_2$ teaspoon kosher salt

Freshly ground black pepper

1 to $1^1/_2$ pounds cod fillet

Juice of 1 lemon

1 cup dry hard cider

2 tablespoons chopped parsley

WHICH BEER?
The same cider used for cooking,
or hefeweizen.

Heat the oil in a large skillet over medium heat. Cook the potatoes until they begin to brown. Add the onions and half the salt and pepper and cook until the onion softens. Meanwhile, preheat the oven to 350°F, season the fish with the remaining salt and pepper and the lemon juice, and lay it in a shallow bake-and-serve dish.

Transfer the potatoes and onions to the baking dish. Deglaze the skillet with the cider and add it to the fish. Sprinkle with parsley, cover with a lid or foil, and bake until the fish and the potatoes are tender, about 30 minutes. Serve from the baking dish.

Cider: After All, This is Apple Country

■

Although it's not beer, fermented apple cider is closer to beer than to wine in terms of alcoholic content and effervescence. In Spain and France, two traditional wine-drinking nations, the northwest regions near the Atlantic are too cool to grow grapes, so the local "wine" is cider, which is bottled either still or lightly sparkling at about half the strength of table wine. England has a particularly rich tradition of hard cider, especially in the western counties, where locally brewed cider—crisp and dry, slightly tannic, and wonderful with seafood—is available on draft in every pub. Some of this tradition came to colonial New England, where hard cider (like ale) was brewed both in the home and commercially.

Somewhere along the line, cider fell out of favor in North America, and I include a section on cider in this book more as wishful thinking than as a real option, because I am disappointed in the state of hard cider brewing in the West. With all the apples grown here, and all the interest in traditional brewing styles, it would seem a natural fit to produce dry ciders in Old World styles. But if someone is doing it, it's either the industry's best-kept secret or its worst publicized product.

Whether it's a matter of timidity on the part of the brewers or an actual response from drinkers, the assumption seems to be that Americans won't buy a truly dry cider. Some nearly dry versions are made in New England, especially the Woodchuck brand from Vermont, but they still don't come as close to the English model as I would like. The most widely available West Coast brands, Ace and Widmer Wildwood, are noticeably sweet, due to the addition after fermenting dry of up to 20 percent unfermented apple juice. (Ace also has a pear-flavored version.)

Despite the current record, I hold on to the hope that someone will take up the challenge of producing a world-class dry cider in the Northwest. For now, even the current sweet ciders have a good backbone of acidity that especially complements seafood (and work well with Thanksgiving dinner and other holiday meals). I have included one recipe that uses cider as a cooking medium (see Cod Baked in Cider, page 45) and another that pairs it with Dungeness crab (see opposite). Either would be better still with a truly dry cider.

Dungeness Crab au Naturel

■ *Serves 2*

It's been nearly twenty years, and I have forgotten the name of the pub (it was in a small town in Dorset, on the edge of the New Forest), but to this day I remember one of the finest combinations of food and drink I have ever had: a good-sized cold cooked crab served with a simple mayonnaise flavored with some of the fat of the crab, and a mug of dry English cider. Heavenly.

I would put our local Dungeness crab up against its English cousin any day. I wish I could say the same about our cider. But even with a sweetish one like Ace, this match works very well. The search goes on.

This is no time to mess around—allow a crab per person. You could serve it as a "salad," as they did in England—which mostly consisted of presenting it on a bed of lettuce—but I'm equally happy with the minimalist approach: crab on a plate, newspaper on the table for the shells. Some good, crusty, whole-grain bread, sourdough if you like, is appropriate in either case.

2 live Dungeness crabs, 1¹/₂ to 2 pounds each

2 tablespoons kosher salt

¹/₄ cup mayonnaise

Dijon or other prepared mustard (optional)

WHICH BEER?
Cider, as dry as you can find.

Place the crabs in a deep pot with cool water to cover by several inches. Add the salt. Cover the pot and bring the water just short of boiling over high heat. Turn off the heat, keep the pot covered, and let steep 15 minutes for small crabs, 18 to 20 minutes for larger ones.

Remove the crabs with tongs and rinse with cold water to stop the cooking. Stand the crabs, eyes facing up, in a bowl and refrigerate until well chilled. To cool the crabs faster, surround them with ice.

Clean the crabs as follows: Working over a bowl or sink, remove and discard the triangular flap or "apron" on the underside, being careful of the spines hidden underneath. Grasp the underside and legs of the crab with one hand and pull off the top shell with the other. Drain off any water and set aside the top shells for now. If there is a layer of whitish fat on top of the body of the crab, taste it; if it is not bitter, scrape it off with a spoon and add it to the top shells. Remove the jaws, the gills (the gray, feathery pieces on each side of the body), and all the spongy stuff in the center of the body. Rinse the crab well until nothing but shell and meat remains.

Taste the fat in the corners of the top shells. If it is not bitter, stir some into the mayonnaise to taste (up to 1 part crab fat to 2 parts mayonnaise). Add a little mustard if you like. (Or set out the plain mayonnaise and mustard for each person to blend to taste.)

Divide and crack the crabs in the kitchen if you like, or else serve them whole with the top shells loosely balanced on top. Provide nutcrackers to get at the meat and individual bowls for the mayonnaise.

Honey Cake with Stout

■ *Serves 16*

*Stout replaces coffee in this version of a traditional Jewish holiday dessert.
It's a dense, homey spice cake, with cardamom sounding the highest note.
The aroma and flavor from the stout get stronger with age, and the texture is
also better on the second day. It will keep for up to four days. Serve plain, or
perhaps with some strawberries or other fresh fruit.*

3$^1/_2$ cups all-purpose flour

2 teaspoons baking powder

$^1/_2$ teaspoon kosher salt

1 teaspoon ground cinnamon

$^1/_2$ teaspoon ground cardamom

$^1/_8$ teaspoon ground cloves

$^1/_8$ teaspoon ground nutmeg

3 eggs

$^1/_2$ cup sugar

2 tablespoons mild vegetable oil

1 cup dark honey

1$^1/_4$ cups dry stout

1 teaspoon powdered sugar

WHICH BEER?

Stout (sweet or dry), barley wine

Preheat the oven to 325°F. Coat an angel-food pan with cooking spray
and dust the inside with flour.

Sift the flour, baking powder, salt, cinnamon, cardamom, cloves, and
nutmeg together into a medium bowl. In a large bowl, using an electric
mixer, beat the eggs and sugar together on high speed until pale yellow
and lightly thickened. Add the oil and honey and beat on medium speed
until smooth. Beat in a third of the dry mixture, then half the stout,
then another third of the dry mixture, then the remaining stout, then
the remaining dry mixture, mixing thoroughly after each addition.
Stop mixing periodically to scrape down the sides of the bowl with a
rubber spatula.

Pour the batter into the prepared pan. Lift the pan an inch off the counter and drop it; repeat twice (to release any large air bubbles). Bake on the middle shelf of the oven until a cake tester comes out clean, 1 hour to 1 hour and 10 minutes. Let cool on a wire rack before removing from the pan. Dust the top with powdered sugar before serving.

PIZZA AND BEYOND:

Beer and the Foods of Mediterranean Europe

Wine may be the favorite beverage from Spain and Portugal through southern France, Italy, and the Balkans to Greece, but the ingredients that shape all the cuisines of southern Europe—olives and their oil, wheat (in bread and pasta), tomatoes, garlic, tangy cheeses often made from sheep's or goat's milk, and herbs like oregano, basil, and thyme—also combine very well with beer. Pizza and beer are no strangers in North America, but fewer beer drinkers may be aware of the popularity of beer and tapas in Madrid and other Spanish cities. And while it may seem heretical to the French, a good hoppy ale can be the perfect thing to accompany a Languedoc-style cassoulet.

Pantry Notes: Mediterranean Europe

OLIVE OIL: I use two types of olive oil on a regular basis, one relatively mild for cooking (usually a big-can brand like Star or Bertolli) and a more flavorful extra virgin olive oil for salad dressings, sauces, and other dishes where you will really taste the oil. There is an amazing variety of the latter on the market, and you don't have to pay top dollar for a good one from Greece, Italy, or Spain, so shop around. Keep all olive oil in a cool place out of sunlight, and use it within a few months after opening.

GARLIC: Look for rock-hard heads of garlic without any soft or sprouting cloves; this can be a tall order some times of the year. If there is a green sprout in the middle of a clove, some cooks claim that cutting it out improves the flavor of the rest. It certainly can't hurt.

GRATING CHEESES: Authentic Parmigiano-Reggiano from Parma, Italy, sets the world standard, with the more regional Grana Padano close behind. Both beat the pants off any domestic "Parmesan," although I do like the aged Asiago made by Stella of Wisconsin. Pecorino Romano is a sharp sheep's-milk cheese with a similar texture. All these cheeses should be grated just before use, and the cut pieces keep well in the refrigerator. If they get too dry, wrap them in a slightly damp paper towel and then in plastic wrap and refrigerate overnight.

Menu: Spanish Tapas

■

Tortilla Española
Squid Stuffed with Ham
Gambas al Ajillo
(Garlic and Red Pepper Shrimp)
Salt Cod Crostini

■

Vegetable Antipasto Platter:
Marinated Artichokes
Roasted Sweet Pepper Strips
Fennel Vinaigrette
Marinated Pan-Roasted Mushrooms

■

Bridgeport IPA, Humboldt Hefeweizen

Dinnertime in Spain is quite late by American standards, and earlier in the evening the bars and cafes are crowded with people gathered for drinks, conversation, and the delicious little dishes knows as tapas. Originally something small (sometimes complimentary) like a slice of ham or a few olives, taken to soften the effect of drinks on an empty stomach, tapas have evolved into a large genre of appetizers and little plates, often small servings of dishes that could just as well be entrées.

While sherry is the most popular drink with tapas in Spain, many Spanish cities have bars that specialize in beer. The tapas approach to dining has become increasingly popular in this country as well, and it made a happy marriage with the brewpub movement in the mid-1990s when Catalán chef Daniel Olivella opened Thirsty Bear Brewing Company in San Francisco, with the city's largest menu of Spanish-style tapas.

Tapas are just as enjoyable at home. Here is a small selection to get you started. Add some plain or marinated olives, good crusty bread, a sharp cheese (especially a Spanish variety like Manchego), and perhaps some of the antipasto-style vegetables on pages 61–64 for a tapas buffet equally suitable to a party or a family dinner.

Tortilla Española

■ *Serves 6 to 8 as an appetizer*

Is this Spanish standard a flat omelet with as many potatoes as it can hold, or a potato cake bound with egg? It really doesn't matter; it's delicious either way. This one leans more toward the omelet end. Most versions use ordinary russet (baking or Idaho type) potatoes, but I prefer the firmer texture of Yukon Gold, which comes in somewhere between a floury russet and a waxy "new" potato and doesn't require the soaking and draining step.

1 pound small to medium potatoes

About 1½ cups olive oil

1 onion, thinly sliced

**Scant teaspoon kosher salt, mixed with freshly ground
black pepper to taste**

6 eggs

WHICH BEER?

When my wife and I go out for beer and tapas, I order pale ale or IPA, she orders hefeweizen, and we're both happy. In other words, offer an assortment of beers if you're serving tapas to a crowd.

Peel the potatoes if the skins are thick; otherwise just scrub them. Slice crosswise about ⅛ inch thick (see the Technique Note). If using russet potatoes, soak the slices briefly in a bowl of cool water; drain and pat dry.

Fill a 10-inch nonstick skillet with oil to a depth of at least ½ inch and heat over medium-high heat until a potato slice sizzles on contact. Add the potato slices one at a time; it's okay if they overlap. Add the onions on top of the potatoes. Reduce the heat to medium and cook, turning the potatoes frequently with a slotted spoon and reversing the layers, until they are tender but not browned. Transfer the slices as they are done to a colander set over a heatproof bowl, and sprinkle them with a little of the salt and pepper. When the last of the potatoes are done, pour all the oil through the colander into the bowl and turn off the heat.

Let the potatoes cool slightly. In a large bowl, beat the eggs with the remaining salt and pepper just until combined. Add the potatoes and stir to combine.

If any potato has stuck to the skillet, wash or scrape it off. Coat the pan generously with 2 to 3 tablespoons of the reserved oil and reheat over medium-high heat until the oil is almost smoking. Add the egg mixture to the pan, spreading the potatoes evenly. As the egg sets, lift the edges with a spatula and tilt the pan to let some of the liquid egg run off into the pan to cook. When the egg is mostly set, loosen the whole omelet with a spatula, then remove the pan from the heat and invert a plate over the pan. Holding the plate securely, quickly flip the whole thing over; the omelet should fall out onto the plate. If any bits stick to the pan, simply scrape them free and add them to the omelet.

Add a little more oil to the pan, return to the heat, and slide the omelet off the plate into the pan. Cook another minute or two, then turn the omelet out onto the plate again and back into the pan. Decide which side of the omelet looks better, and either slide or turn the omelet back onto the plate for serving. Serve immediately, or let it cool to tepid or room temperature. Cut into wedges or squares to serve.

VARIATION Ham, chorizo, peppers, and other recurring ingredients in Spanish cuisine are frequently added to a tortilla española. Try any combination of the following, stirred into the egg before adding the potatoes:

■ 1 ounce sliced prosciutto or similar dry-cured ham, cut into short strips

■ 1 or 2 roasted and peeled red bell peppers, diced

TECHNIQUE NOTE Don't skimp on the oil in the first step of cooking the potatoes; the idea is to gently fry the potatoes, turning and separating them as you go so they cook evenly. Most of the oil will be left behind, and the flavor it picks up from the potatoes and onions makes it perfect for other sautéed dishes.

Uniform slices of potato and onion are not as crucial here as they are in a gratin, because you can pull the thinner slices out of the oil ahead of the thicker. But for both ease and consistency, try slicing both with a mandoline or the 4-millimeter slicing disc of a food processor.

Squid Stuffed with Ham

■ *Serves 4 to 6 as an appetizer*

An intensely flavored, dry-cured ham like Spanish serrano, Italian prosciutto, or American Smithfield goes wonderfully with the sweet taste of shellfish. Here it combines with garlicky bread crumbs as a stuffing for squid. Because the stuffing is on the dry side, I skip the usual pastry bag technique and simply roll the other ingredients in a thin slice of ham and then pop the whole assembly inside.

2 tablespoons olive oil

½ cup minced onion

2 cloves garlic, minced

1 tablespoon chopped parsley

1 tablespoon dry bread crumbs

**2 ounces dry-cured ham, sliced thin but
   not paper-thin**

1 pound squid, cleaned

¼ cup tomato sauce

Heat 1 tablespoon of the oil in a skillet over low heat. Add the onion and cook until soft but not browned. Add the garlic and parsley and cook another minute or so, just to take the raw edge off the garlic. Transfer the contents of the skillet to a bowl and stir in the bread crumbs. Let cool.

Cut the ham into pieces about two thirds of the length of your squid bodies. Top each slice with some of the bread-crumb mixture, roll it slightly to hold the filling, and insert it into a squid. Tuck one of the tentacle clusters into the opening of each stuffed squid, then run a toothpick through it crosswise to close the opening and trap the tentacles.

Heat the remaining 1 tablespoon oil in the skillet over medium-high heat and cook the squid until they begin to shrink and turn opaque white, about 2 minutes on the first side. Turn, add the tomato sauce, and cook another 2 minutes. Transfer the stuffed squid to a plate, remove the toothpicks, and spoon the sauce over all. If you have any leftover ham, cut it into thin slivers and scatter it over the dish.

Gambas al Ajillo
(Garlic and Red Pepper Shrimp)

■ *Serves 2 to 4 as an appetizer*

One of the most basic shellfish tapas, and one of the best, is large shrimp sautéed in garlicky olive oil with a touch of hot red pepper. If you can get fresh shrimp (often called prawns in the West), by all means use them; otherwise look for good-sized frozen white shrimp, which I much prefer in flavor to the prettier but blander black tiger variety.

8 ounces medium to large raw shrimp
(31–40 size or larger)

2 teaspoons kosher salt

2 tablespoons olive oil

1 large clove garlic, sliced

Pinch of red pepper flakes

1 tablespoon lemon juice

A few minutes to a few hours before cooking, peel and devein the shrimp. In a small bowl, toss the shrimp with a teaspoon of the salt, and let stand 1 minute, then cover with cold water and drain; repeat with the remaining salt, rinsing well and letting the shrimp drain in a colander. Refrigerate until ready to cook.

Combine the oil and garlic in a medium skillet and warm over low heat until the garlic is fragrant and beginning to color. Add the shrimp and pepper flakes, turn the heat to medium, and cook until the shrimp are opaque, 2 to 3 minutes per side. Add the lemon juice and serve in a shallow serving dish or in individual dishes, with crusty bread for dipping in the sauce.

TECHNIQUE NOTE Don't be alarmed by the amount of salt in the recipe; most of it washes away, leaving behind shrimp with a cleaner flavor and a slightly firmer texture. It's a step I always recommend with frozen shrimp, and it doesn't hurt with fresh shrimp either.

Salt Cod Crostini

■ *Serves 6 to 8 as an appetizer*

One of the oldest commodities traded between southern and northern Europe is dried cod from the cold waters of the North Atlantic. Viking traders had already been shipping air-dried cod (stockfisk) to the Mediterranean for centuries before Portuguese and Basque fishermen began to cross the Atlantic to the rich cod grounds off New England and Newfoundland. Using the salt they brought with them (a scarce commodity in the north, which is why the Norwegians developed their air-dried version), the Iberian fishermen split and salted their catch to preserve it for the trip home. Bacalao, bacalhau, or baccalá, as salt cod is known in Spanish, Portuguese, and Italian respectively, remains a favorite traditional food in many Mediterranean countries, although some prefer the unsalted Nordic version.

Probably the best introduction to salt cod is in the French brandade de morue, *a warm purée enriched with milk and olive oil. Because it is so rich, a little* brandade *goes a long way, spread on plain crackers or toasted slices of bread.*

Brandade is traditionally mixed by hand in the skillet, but an electric mixer (either the stand type or hand-held) does the job much more easily. A food processor is less suitable, as it purées everything too far and too fast.

Note that you need to start the brandade *two days before you plan to serve it.*

1 pound salt cod fillet

³/₄ cup olive oil, plus more for brushing crostini

2 to 3 cloves garlic, smashed

1 cup milk

Kosher salt and freshly ground black pepper

Pinch of nutmeg

1 baguette, sliced diagonally ¹/₄ inch thick

At least two days ahead of serving, rinse the fish and cut it into manageable pieces (it may be necessary to let it soak briefly before cutting).

Place the pieces in a glass or other nonreactive dish and cover with cold water. Soak the fish for 24 to 36 hours in the refrigerator, changing the water several times a day.

When you're ready to serve the fish, drain it and place it in a skillet with cold water to cover. Bring slowly to a simmer and poach until the fish flakes. Drain and transfer to a cutting board. Remove and discard any skin and bones, pulling the fish apart into flakes and inspecting it carefully for small bones.

Warm half the oil in a large skillet over medium-low heat. Add the garlic and cook until fragrant. Add the fish and cook 5 minutes, stirring and mashing it with a wooden spoon until it is reduced to small pieces. Transfer the contents of the skillet to a mixing bowl and beat on medium speed until the fish is broken up into fine shreds. Meanwhile, heat the remaining oil in the skillet and bring the milk just to a boil in a small saucepan.

With the mixer running on low speed, alternately add hot oil and hot milk to the purée, allowing a few seconds for each addition to be fully absorbed. (Transferring the oil and milk to heatproof measuring cups with pouring spouts will make the job easier.) Continue adding oil and milk until the mixture reaches a creamy, spreadable consistency (you may not need all the oil and milk). Season to taste with pepper and nutmeg; if the fish has been thoroughly desalted, some salt may also be needed. Serve warm, or refrigerate and reheat slowly in a double boiler to serve.

Preheat the oven to 350°F. Brush the baguette slices lightly with olive oil, or spray with a mister filled with olive oil, and place them on a baking sheet. Toast in the oven until lightly browned. Let cool or serve warm from the oven, spread with a little brandade.

VARIATION Norwegian-style stockfish will also work, if it is easier to come by than salt cod. Because it has no salt, stockfish is much drier and should be given several days longer to rehydrate (up to a week is typical in Norway).

Vegetable Antipasto Platter

■ *Each will serve 3 or 4 by itself, more as part of an assortment*

Beer drinkers need to eat their veggies, and a chicken-topped Caesar salad now and then won't do. Here is an assortment of Mediterranean-style vegetable dishes that can be served cold or at room temperature, as an appetizer or salad, as Italian-style antipasto (which means before the meal, not before the pasta), with tapas, as part of a buffet . . . you get the picture.

Marinated Artichokes

■

3 or 4 medium artichokes, or 1½ pounds egg-size "baby" artichokes (sometimes inaccurately labeled "hearts")

1 tablespoon plus 1 teaspoon vinegar

1 teaspoon kosher salt

½ bay leaf

¼ cup sliced onion

1 clove garlic

½ teaspoon peppercorns

¼ teaspoon fennel seeds

2 tablespoons olive oil

WHICH BEER?
As with other appetizers, a good hefeweizen or dry-finishing pale ale.

Have a bowl of water acidulated with 1 tablespoon vinegar standing by. If using medium to large artichokes, the kind sold by the piece rather than the pound, bend back the outer leaves of an artichoke until they break easily, leaving a little of the base of each leaf attached. Continue until the leaves are more yellow than green, then slice off the green tops. Trim away the dark green outer part of the stem and base. Dip the freshly cut surfaces in acidulated water as you work, to reduce browning. Repeat with the remaining artichokes, then cut the trimmed wholes into halves or quarters. Remove the fuzzy chokes and spiny-tipped inner leaves with a knife or melon scoop and discard.

With "baby" artichokes, simply snap off the outer leaves at their bases until you get down to leaves that are more yellow than green, then slice off the top third and trim the bases as described above. Halve or quarter the artichokes (depending on their size) and inspect the centers; if the chokes are very small and tender, you can leave them in, but cut them out if they look fuzzy enough to be unpleasant to eat.

Put the trimmed artichokes in a stainless or other nonreactive saucepan with water just to cover. Add the remaining ingredients, bring to a boil, reduce to a simmer, and cook until the artichokes are tender, 10 to 15 minutes, depending on their size. Remove the artichokes from the liquid to a bowl or serving dish. Boil down the liquid to about ½ cup and strain it over the artichokes. Refrigerate if not serving the same day. Serve warm, cool, or at room temperature.

Roasted Sweet Pepper Strips

■

Red, yellow, orange, or green bell peppers

Olive oil for drizzling

Kosher salt and freshly ground black pepper

Wash the peppers and drain well. Cut each pepper vertically along the indentations from the bottoms to near the stems. Break away the sections, 3 or 4 per pepper, leaving the stems and most of the seeds behind. Trim the ribs from the edges of each section. Place cut side down in a roasting pan, drizzle with a little olive oil, then turn skin side down. Roast in a 400°F oven (no need to wait for it to preheat) until the peppers are mostly collapsed and the skins are browned and blistered. Remove from the oven and let cool in the pan. Peel off and discard the skins and cut the pepper flesh into strips. If the combined oil and juices in the pan are not burnt, swirl the pepper strips around in the pan to pick up their flavor. Season with a little salt and pepper if you like, though none is really necessary.

Marinated Pan-Roasted Mushrooms

■

1/4 cup olive oil

2 cloves garlic, sliced

1 pound medium to large mushrooms, white or brown

Kosher salt and freshly ground black pepper

2 tablespoons sherry vinegar or balsamic vinegar, or to taste

Combine the oil and garlic in a medium mixing bowl. Wash the mushrooms only if absolutely necessary; otherwise just brush away any dirt and debris. Snap off the stems and discard, or save for another use. Toss the caps in the bowl with the oil and a generous pinch of salt and pepper. They will probably absorb most of the oil, and unevenly; that's okay. Set aside until ready to cook, up to a couple of hours.

Heat a large, dry skillet or flat-bottomed wok over medium-high heat. Add as many mushrooms as will fit in a single layer, gill sides up. As they begin to shrink, water will pool up in the middles. Turn and continue cooking, gills down, until tender. Total cooking time is 8 to 10 minutes; add more mushrooms to the pan as space becomes available.

Transfer the cooked mushrooms back to the bowl and sprinkle with the vinegar. Let cool before serving. Serve at room temperature within 3 or 4 days.

Fennel Vinaigrette

■

1 bulb fresh fennel, about 12 ounces

1 teaspoon good wine vinegar

1/2 teaspoon Dijon-style mustard

Kosher salt and freshly ground black pepper

1 tablespoon extra virgin olive oil

Trim off the top of the bulb where it begins to branch, and discard any beat-up outer layers. Split the bulb vertically, then slice crosswise about

⅛ inch thick. (For a milder flavor, steam the bulb halves for 3 to 5 minutes before slicing.)

Combine the vinegar, mustard, and a good pinch of salt and pepper in a mixing bowl and whisk or mix with your fingertips to dissolve the salt. Whisk in the oil, taste a bit of the dressing on a slice of fennel, and adjust the flavors to taste. Toss the fennel slices in the dressing and serve cool or at room temperature.

NOTE Fresh fennel (called sweet anise in some markets) combines the texture of celery with a sweet licorice flavor. It is available most of the year but is generally best and least expensive from fall to spring. The "bulbs" are actually the thick bases of the stalks, extending 4 to 6 inches above the soil level until they branch into tough green stems topped with feathery leaves. For maximum flavor, use fennel raw; if you want to tone the flavor down slightly, cook it briefly.

VARIATION Omit the mustard and add 1 or 2 canned anchovy fillets, rinsed and chopped, to the dressing before adding the fennel. Go a little easier on the salt in this case.

Pizza

■ *Makes four 11-inch or three 12-inch rounds, or two 11-by 17-inch rectangles*

It's no accident that many brewpubs are also pizzerias. Both brewing and baking involve grain and yeast (though not the same grains nor the same yeast) in a process that is part hands-on and part patience, ultimately transforming basic ingredients into something delicious. And the two end products go very well together.

Of course, you can top homemade pizza with standard stuff like thick tomato sauce, mozzarella, sausage, pepperoni, and mushrooms, but if you are going to make your own, why not make something you can't get at every pizzeria? A few of my favorites follow.

1 tablespoon (1 package) active dry yeast

1½ cups warm (100°F) water

¼ cup rye or whole wheat flour

About 4 cups all-purpose flour

1½ tablespoons olive oil

2 teaspoons kosher salt

Cornmeal or coarse semolina flour, for dusting

Pizza toppings (recipes follow)

WHICH BEER?

What beer doesn't go with pizza, and vice versa? The only thing to watch out for is serving very highly hopped, dry-finishing ales with hot stuff like pepperoni. See the individual pizza toppings for more specific ideas.

Dissolve the yeast in the water in a large mixing bowl, or in the bowl of a stand mixer. When it begins to bubble, stir in the rye flour and 1½ cups of the all-purpose flour. Beat 100 strokes by hand or 2 minutes at low speed in the mixer. Cover the bowl with plastic wrap and let the batter rise in a warm place until bubbly, 45 minutes to an hour or more.

When the sponge is nice and bubbly, stir in the oil and salt and another cup or two of flour. Mix as thoroughly as possible in the bowl, then turn the dough out onto a floured surface. Knead in as much of the remaining flour as needed to make a smooth dough. Oil the bowl and return the dough to the bowl, turning it to oil all sides evenly. Cover and allow the dough to rise until doubled in bulk, about 1 hour.

In the Hop Zone: West Coast Pale Ales

■

If there is one style of beer that typifies West Coast craft brewing, it would have to be pale ale. From the earliest days of the West Coast homebrew boom, English ales like Bass and the myriad brands of "bitter" served in English pubs provided an attractive model for brewers in search of more flavor. These ales had more color (a coppery or amber tone that is only "pale" in comparison to darker ales like stout and porter), more malty and estery flavors, and above all more hop aroma and bitterness than any domestic beer could offer. (Not to mention the fact that ales are easier and faster to brew than lagers—see page 7.)

With typical American more-is-better enthusiasm, homebrewers and early microbreweries went for the more pronounced versions of the style, known in England as best bitter, ESB (extra special bitter), or India pale ale. (The last label dates to the late colonial period, for a style of ale brewed stronger and more highly hopped to survive shipping to the farthest parts of the Empire.) Many took it a step or two further, using even more hops than most English ales. The style has remained popular, and except for those that specialize in lagers, it's hard to think of a West Coast craft brewery that does not offer a pale ale, perhaps under a related label like IPA, ESB, or bitter.

West Coast pale ale is typically amber in color, with a thick white head (most are more carbonated than typical English ales), a pronounced hop aroma and bitterness, and a touch of sweetness but a dry finish. Classic examples of the style abound; among my favorites are Sierra Nevada Pale Ale, Mendocino Brewing's Red Tail Ale, Anchor Steam Beer and Liberty Ale, Redhook ESB, and Pike Pale. (Anchor Steam is technically a lager, but its warm fermentation and strong hop content give it a flavor profile more like that of a pale ale.)

Pale ales often appeal to the same people who enjoy full-flavored red wines like cabernet, zinfandel, and syrah, and they complement many of the same foods. Like the tannins in these wines, the hop bitterness (which includes some tannin) provides good balance to rich, meaty foods, cutting the fatty feel on the palate. Lamb, pork roast with prunes, smoked meat dishes (try it with Cassoulet, page 73), smoky grilled salmon, and pizza are just a few of my favorite pale ale partners.

Punch down the dough and divide it into 4, 3, or 2 pieces, depending on the desired size. With lightly floured hands, form each piece of dough into a ball, stretching the top slightly as you tuck the sides under, and finishing by rolling it around on the board with one hand until the top surface is smooth. Place the balls on a floured tray at least 2 inches apart, cover with a towel, and let them rest for at least 30 minutes and up to 4 hours. (Or cover with plastic wrap and refrigerate overnight; allow at least 1 hour for the refrigerated dough to return to room temperature before forming the pizzas.)

Preheat the oven to 450°F, with a pizza stone or baking tiles on the lowest rack. Have your topping ingredients ready, and dust a baker's peel or a rimless cookie sheet with fine cornmeal or semolina. To form round pizzas by hand, place a ball of dough on a lightly floured surface and press it gently with the fingertips into a disk about twice the original diameter. Lift the far edge of the circle and, holding it between your fingertips and the heels of your hands, gently stretch it to increase the diameter of the edge. Work your way around the edge, letting the weight of the dough stretch the middle, until you have a large circle with a thin center and a thicker edge.

The next step is harder to describe than it is to do: Drape the far edge of dough over one wrist, letting that hand curl inward in a relaxed position. Holding the near edge with your other hand, stretch the dough gently against the curved wrist, then give it a little flip to rotate it 90 to 120 degrees. Repeat, stretching the next part of the edge. One or two more flips should produce a nice circle 11 inches or so across.

Lay the circle of dough on the prepared peel, stretching a little dough back toward the center if necessary to close any tears. Add your choice of toppings. Slide the pizza directly onto the baking stone and bake until the edges are golden brown and the bottom is crisp and browned, about 12 minutes; use a long-bladed spatula to rotate the pizza halfway though the cooking time so it bakes evenly. Brush the edge of the finished pizza with a little more olive oil if you like.

TECHNIQUE NOTE To make a rectangular pizza on a baking sheet, roll and press half the dough into an 11- by 17-inch rimmed baking pan as for Focaccia (page 72), but skip the extra oil and final rising and add your favorite pizza toppings.

VARIATIONS

Pesto, Potato, and Pancetta

Put some small, thin-skinned potatoes in the oven to roast while it preheats. Coarsely chop 2 slices of pancetta or bacon and cook in a skillet until they render some of their fat; you can also do this in another small pan in the oven. Brush each 11-inch dough round with a scant 2 tablespoons pesto (page 92), top with slices of potato (which may be only partly cooked at this stage; that's okay), and scatter the drained pancetta pieces around the potato. Try this pizza with pale ale, porter, or stout.

Margherita

In authentic Neapolitan style, this is a rather sparsely topped pizza, with more crust showing between the tomatoes and cheese than most Americans would expect. Lightly salt slices of fresh tomato, preferably cherry or plum size, and set aside to drain for a few minutes. Arrange the drained slices on the pizza dough, add some 1/4-inch slices of fresh fior di latte mozzarella, and finish with a drizzle of olive oil. Top with basil leaves after baking. I like Märzen or amber ale with this.

Shrimp, Tomato, and Feta

Brush each 11-inch pizza with 1 tablespoon extra virgin olive oil, and scatter on a scant teaspoon of chopped garlic, then 1/2 cup peeled, seeded, and sliced tomato, 1/4 cup crumbled feta cheese, and 4 ounces small raw shrimp, peeled and coarsely chopped. Sprinkle with chopped fresh herbs (marjoram, oregano, thyme, or Italian parsley) and a little more olive oil after baking. Try it with hefeweizen.

Onion, Anchovy, and Olive

This pizza is a variation on pissaladière, the Provençal leek tart. Quarter 1 large onion through the root end and slice the quarters thinly crosswise. Cook gently in 2 tablespoons olive oil to a pale golden color. Spread the onions over the pizza dough, top with rinsed anchovy fillets (whole or roughly chopped) and kalamata or niçoise olives. Definitely a pale ale pizza.

Pizza Tools and Techniques

■

There's nothing especially tricky about making pizza at home. If you can make a bread dough, you can make a pizza dough. While it takes practice to make perfectly shaped pizzas consistently, even the lumpiest, most pear-shaped pizza has its charm (and tastes good). If you absolutely can't get the hang of shaping pizzas by hand, you can always roll them out with a rolling pin and accept the somewhat denser crust that results.

The recipe for pizza dough here makes enough for 4 small pizzas, which may be more than you need. The extra dough makes great breadsticks, or you can shape it into a round or oval loaf of *pane all'olio* (olive oil bread).

A few special tools are helpful to home pizza cooks though not essential. All of them are also useful for baking rustic breads. A pizza stone, a large flat square or circle of unglazed ceramic, turns the bottom shelf of an oven into something like the brick floor of traditional pizza ovens, and makes an especially crisp crust. I use a square of four 6-inch unglazed quarry tiles, which are available and cheap at any tile shop and most building-supply stores, but this limits me to 11-inch pizzas. A baker's peel, a big flat hardwood paddle with a narrow edge, is handy for assembling the pizza and sliding it onto the stone (but not for getting it out again, which will scrape up and burn your peel in short order). Lacking a peel, you can use a rimless cookie sheet for the same purpose. I draw the line at a pizza spatula, which is essentially a metal version of the peel used for getting pizzas and breads out of the oven; the same large offset spatula I use for grilled fish fillets works fine.

If you don't have all this stuff, you can still make delicious pizzas on an ordinary baking sheet, set on the lowest rack of the oven to get the most heat underneath.

What to Do with Extra Pizza Dough

■

If you're going to go to the trouble of making pizza dough and heating up the oven, you might as well get more than one meal out of it. Here are two options for roughly half a batch of pizza dough, starting with a good crusty loaf of bread that can cook on the same tiles after the pizza comes out.

Pane all'Olio (Olive Oil Bread)

■ *Makes 1 small loaf*

This oval loaf bakes on the same surface as the pizza but at a slightly lower temperature and with some moisture added to the oven.

¹/₂ recipe Pizza Dough (page 65)

Prepare the dough through the first rise, punching down, and dividing steps. Instead of a ball, form the dough into an oval about 9 inches long. Lay a clean, dry kitchen towel on a sheet pan and dust one end with flour. Lay the dough on the floured end, dust the top of the loaf with more flour, and fold the towel loosely over it. Let rise 20 to 30 minutes in a warm place. Preheat the oven to 350°F and place a shallow metal pan of water (such as a pie tin) on the oven floor under the rack with the tiles.

Dust a peel or rimless cookie sheet with cornmeal or semolina. Roll the loaf, still wrapped in its towel, over on its top, then use the towel to invert it onto the peel. With a very sharp knife or razor blade, make a single lengthwise slash in the top. Slide the loaf off the peel onto the stone and bake until the bottom is nicely browned and sounds hollow when thumped, 35 to 45 minutes. Let cool on a rack before storing or slicing.

Grissini (Breadsticks)

Breadsticks are probably the simplest way to use leftover pizza dough—once you get the hang of shaping them—but they are also the least likely to last. Prepare the dough through the first rising and punch it down. Shape whatever dough you will not be using for pizza into a long oval like French bread, as even as possible in diameter (the length is less important). Lay it on a floured sheet pan, brush the top with a little more oil, and let it rise until doubled, about an hour.

Line one or more sheet pans with baking parchment. Brush the loaf once more with olive oil. With a bench scraper or a knife, slice the loaf crosswise about $1/4$ inch thick, making short, irregular slices. (You will knock a lot of the air out in the process; that's okay.) Holding a strip of dough with both hands meeting near the middle, gently stretch the dough with a bit of a swinging action as you work your hands out toward the ends, and finish by rolling the ends between thumbs and fingers to match the diameter of the middle. The goal is to make sticks about 9 inches long and as consistent in thickness as possible; pay more attention to diameter than to length. Lay the stretched pieces $1/4$ inch apart on the lined baking pans. Let the breadsticks rise for about 15 minutes while preheating the oven to 375°F. Bake until golden brown and crisp, 8 to 10 minutes. Let cool before serving.

VARIATION For cheese-flavored grissini, dust the top of the loaf with 1/4 cup grated Parmesan, Romano, Asiago, or similar cheese just before slicing. Drag the slices through any excess cheese lying on the pan before stretching.

Focaccia

■ *Makes one 11-by 17-inch sheet*

What we know as pizza probably evolved from focaccia, a flat bread baked directly on the hearth (focus in Latin). In its modern form, focaccia is a thick, light, yeast-risen bread enriched with olive oil, with toppings ranging from simple coarse salt or chopped herbs to some rather pizzalike creations with tomatoes, onions, or artichoke hearts. Cheese, if used at all, should be just a minimal dusting of Parmesan or something similar. Plain focaccia split lengthwise also makes a delicious sandwich bread.

The dough is basically the same as for pizza, but for some reason the bit of rye or whole wheat flour that improves pizza does nothing for focaccia.

Pizza Dough (page 65), made without the rye or whole wheat flour

2 tablespoons extra virgin olive oil

½ teaspoon kosher salt

1 tablespoon chopped fresh rosemary

Prepare the dough through the first rise, and punch it down. Turn the dough out onto an 11- by 17-inch rimmed baking pan (a standard baker's half-sheet or jelly roll pan). With lightly floured hands, gently flatten the dough, stretching it out toward the edges of the pan. Use a rolling pin only if necessary; this may be impossible anyway if your pan has a deep rim. The goal is to fill the pan to the edges with as even a layer of dough as possible. Cover the pan and let rise until doubled, 1 to 2 hours in a warm place or overnight in the refrigerator.

Preheat the oven to 400°F. Dimple the top of the focaccia with slight fingertip impressions every inch or so, then brush with the oil. Sprinkle the salt and rosemary over the top and bake on an upper rack of the oven until golden brown and crisp on the bottom, about 20 minutes. It's a good idea to rotate the pan halfway through cooking, as many ovens heat unevenly from front to back.

VARIATION Instead of rosemary, top the focaccia with thickly sliced green onions just before baking.

Cassoulet

▪ *Serves 6 to 8*

I include this recipe with a certain amount of trepidation, as cassoulet is one of those traditional dishes that arouses strong opinions about what it should or should not contain. Various cities in its native Languedoc region of southwest France have their own authentic, "original" versions, all based on beans slowly baked with a rich assortment of meats and poultry. I don't know if the French would approve of this version, let alone the idea of serving it with beer rather than red wine. But I serve it with pride, and my family and friends love it.

Note that you need to make the duck confit a few days ahead, unless you can buy it already made (a possibility in some areas). Remember also to soak the beans the night before, or else use the quick-soaking method in the first step.

2 cups dried white beans (French flageolet, Great Northern, cannellini, or navy)

About 4 cups unsalted chicken or duck stock

2 small onions, peeled and halved through the root ends

2 medium carrots, peeled and halved

1 head garlic, halved crosswise

2 thick slices bacon or pancetta

1 inner celery stalk, with leaves

3 or 4 sprigs parsley

1 large sprig thyme

1 bay leaf

12 ounces mild pork sausages (preferably made without fennel seeds)

3 or 4 legs duck or chicken confit (page 75), or a mixture of legs, wings, and gizzards (see Note)

$^1/_3$ cup unseasoned dried bread crumbs

WHICH BEER?

This is a perfect demonstration of the way a highly hopped ale complements rich foods. Where a malty amber might seem heavy on the palate, the high hop bitterness of a pale ale or IPA cuts through the feel of fat on the palate, setting you up for another taste.

One day ahead:

Pick over the beans and discard any stones or discolored beans. Rinse, drain, and cover with cold water. Soak overnight. Quick-soaking method: If starting the same day you plan to serve, sort and rinse the beans, cover with cold water in a pot, bring to a boil, turn off the heat, and let steep 1 hour before proceeding.

Four to six hours ahead of serving:

Drain and rinse the beans. Place in a large pot and add stock to cover by about ½ inch. Bring to a simmer over medium heat. While the stock warms, prepare and add the onions, carrots, garlic, and bacon. Bundle the celery, parsley, thyme, and bay leaf together, tying them with kitchen twine, and add to the pot. Simmer, partially covered, until the beans are tender, 1 to 2 hours, depending on the variety and freshness. (The beans may be a little grainy at this point, but if they are still crunchy let them cook a little longer, or plan on longer cooking in the oven.) Whenever it is convenient during this time, add the sausages to the pot and simmer just until firm; retrieve and set aside. Set the confit container out in a warm place for the fat to soften.

Preheat the oven to 250°F. Drain the beans through a colander, reserving the broth. Return the broth to the pot, bring to a boil, and reduce by half. Meanwhile, discard the bacon, vegetables, and herb bundle from the beans. Recombine the broth and beans, taste for seasoning, and add a little salt if necessary (bearing in mind the salt in the sausage and confit).

Remove the confit from its fat, scraping off as much as possible. Brown the legs slightly (the pot you used for the beans is fine for this, if it has a heavy bottom), transfer to a cutting board, and divide them into drumsticks and thighs. Slice the sausages about 1/2 inch thick and brown in the same pan.

Choose a 2-quart or larger baking dish, on the deep side. Spread a third of the beans in the dish, top with half the sausage slices, then more beans and sausage, then the rest of the beans with their broth. Arrange the confit portions on top, pushing them down slightly into the beans. Sprinkle the bread crumbs over the top, mostly over the beans, and drizzle the crumbs with a tablespoon or so of the confit fat (either from the crock or from browning the sausage). Bake until the crust is golden brown and the beans have absorbed most of the broth, about 2 hours. Serve from the baking dish.

NOTE If you present this as a bean dish accented with meats, rather than a meat dish that includes beans, then everyone won't expect to get a whole drumstick or thigh. If you prefer the latter, feel free to use more confit, as well as other meats listed in the variation below. Just make sure you have room in your baking dish for most of the confit to brown on top.

I'm too frugal (and I like poultry wings too much) to consign duck wings to the stockpot, so I include them in my confit, along with the gizzards. That way, confit made from one duck (two legs halved, two wings, and one halved gizzard) is just enough for 6 servings.

If there is a French-style sausage maker in your area, try to find Toulouse-style sausages, a slightly sweet variety flavored with nutmeg or mace. The strong fennel flavor found in most Italian sausage is out of place in an authentic cassoulet.

VARIATION Substitute a ham hock for the bacon in the first cooking of the beans; you can incorporate some of the meat into the cassoulet or save the whole thing for another meal. In either case, the ham hock should provide plenty of salt. Other meats that can be added to the cassoulet include cubes of braised fresh pork, leftover cooked lamb, or cooked poultry giblets (gizzards and hearts, but not livers) retrieved from making stock.

Duck Confit

■

Confit is a French term for meats and poultry seasoned with salt, simmered slowly in their own fat, and stored in the same fat. When reheated and well drained, the result is rich but not greasy and both more intense in flavor and more tender than the same meats cooked by other methods. Like many traditional foods, confit began as a way to preserve meat before refrigeration, and with sufficient salt confit can keep for months at cellar temperatures. These days, it's typically salted somewhat less and stored in the refrigerator.

Duck and goose are the most common forms of poultry used for confit, and most chefs wouldn't bother with anything as pedestrian as chicken.

However, the technique remains a good way to "put up" an excess of chicken legs for use a week or so later, and it does transform the flavor and texture into something much more interesting than plain cooked chicken (see the variation following the recipe).

4 duck legs

2 tablespoons kosher salt

$1/4$ teaspoon freshly ground black pepper

1 clove garlic, minced

$1/4$ teaspoon dried thyme leaves, or 1 teaspoon fresh

1 bay leaf

Pinch of ground cloves

$2^1/2$ to 3 cups rendered duck or chicken fat, or a combination

Trim any excess skin and fat from the legs and save it for rendering. Combine the salt, pepper, garlic, herbs, and cloves and rub generously over the meat and skin. Let stand in a covered bowl in the refrigerator overnight or for up to 2 days.

Preheat the oven to 200°F. Choose a covered baking dish just big enough to fit the legs snugly. Put the fat in the dish and set it in the oven to melt as the oven warms. Rinse any visible salt off the legs, drain well, and pat dry.

When the fat has melted, slide the legs into the baking dish, cover, and bake until the meat is very tender and almost but not quite falling off the bone, about 2 hours.

Remove the legs from the pan and place them in a deep container (a crock is traditional, but an 8-cup soufflé dish or a very large glass jar also works). Let the liquid contents of the pan cool slightly, then pour into a 2-quart heatproof measuring pitcher. Strain in any drippings that have accumulated in the crock containing the legs. Let stand until the meat juices (there may be as much as a cup) settle below the fat. Carefully pour the fat over the legs, covering them completely. When the juices are about to reach the pouring spout, stop pouring and either draw out the juices with a bulb baster before proceeding or carefully ladle the fat off the top and into the crock. The idea is to get as little of the juices as possible in the crock. (Save the juices to use in the cassoulet, or wherever you can use some flavorful salted stock.)

Cover the crock and refrigerate for up to a week. To use, remove the crock from the refrigerator and set it in a warm place (or set it in warm water) until the fat softens enough to pull out as many pieces as you need. Scrape the excess fat back into the crock and return the crock to the refrigerator. Reheat the confit in a double boiler or steamer, then drain the melted fat back into the crock.

NOTE Wings and gizzards also make good confit, though not as meaty. Use only the upper wing section, or the upper and middle as you like. Increase the seasonings by half if you will be adding the wings and gizzards to the confit.

VARIATION
Chicken Confit

Substitute chicken legs (and upper wing sections) for the duck. Try using chicken confit in a warm salad like the one on page 192, or in place of duck in Cassoulet (page 73).

Rosemary-Crusted Rack of Lamb

■ *Serves 4 to 6*

Like prime rib roast beef or the rib end of a pork loin, cuts to which it is anatomically identical, rack of lamb provides the perfect combination of tenderness and flavor, making it ideal for cooking by dry heat. Rack of lamb can be simply roasted, but searing it first in a hot skillet (which I learned from The Complete Meat Cookbook *by Bruce Aidells and Denis Kelly) gives it more of a browned flavor and crusty exterior.*

WHICH BEER?

IPA or other pale ale; possibly a dry porter or stout.

2 racks of lamb, about 1$\frac{1}{2}$ pounds each

1 heaping tablespoon fresh rosemary leaves

1 clove garlic

2 tablespoons dried bread crumbs

Kosher salt and freshly ground black pepper

About 2 tablespoons olive oil

$\frac{1}{2}$ cup red wine

$\frac{1}{2}$ cup unsalted beef, veal, or lamb stock

Trim the excess fat from the side of the racks opposite the bones; for the easiest eating and the leanest cut, remove the entire "cap," the thin flap of meat spreading out parallel to the rib bones, as well as all the attached fat. For Frenched racks, cut crosswise down to the bone about 1½ inches in from the tips, then cut between the bones to remove all the meat between the bones from there out to the tips.

Chop the rosemary and garlic together finely (by hand or in a food processor) and combine with the bread crumbs, a pinch of salt and pepper, and 1 tablespoon olive oil. Spread the mixture on a plate or in a shallow bowl.

Preheat the oven to 475°F. Season the lamb with salt and pepper. Heat a heavy cast-iron or stainless skillet (you can do this in the oven; just remember that the handle will get hot). Coat the skillet with a thin film of oil and brown the racks for a few minutes on a side, first with the bone side up and then on the edge, with the bones held vertically. Remove the racks as they are done and add some of the lamb trimmings to the skillet.

Press the meat side of the racks into the bread crumb mixture, and place them bones down in a roasting pan. Fill in any bare spots with the remaining crumb coating. Roast to an internal temperature of 125°F for rare, 130° to 140°F for medium-rare.

While the racks are roasting, prepare the pan sauce: When the lamb trimmings in the skillet are browned nicely, push them to the side and swab out as much fat as possible with a paper towel. Add the wine and bring to a boil, stirring to deglaze the pan. Add the stock and boil until reduced by half.

When the racks come out of the oven, transfer them to a cutting board and let rest for a few minutes before carving. If the drippings in the roasting pan are not too burnt, deglaze the pan with the contents of the skillet, adding a little more water or stock if needed to keep it from boiling dry. Strain the sauce, let it stand until the fat rises to the top, and discard the fat. Correct the seasoning.

To serve, slice the racks crosswise into single or double chops, allowing 3 to 4 ribs per serving. Serve on warmed plates, with a little of the pan sauce spooned around the meat.

Green Beans with Garlic Oil

■ *Serves 4*

These beans make a great accompaniment to lamb, roast chicken, roast beef, and a whole lot of other meat dishes. Store the extra garlic-flavored oil in the refrigerator and use within a week or so.

4 large cloves garlic, peeled

1/4 cup oil (peanut or mild olive)

1 pound green beans

Slice the garlic cloves crosswise quite thinly; consistency is more important than the thinnest slices. Combine the slices and oil in a small saucepan and set over very low heat. Cook, stirring occasionally to separate the slices, until they are a rich golden brown. Do not let them brown too much or too fast, or they will become bitter. Strain through a fine wire sieve set over a heatproof bowl.

Trim the beans, splitting them lengthwise if on the large side. Cut to the desired size. Bring a pot of lightly salted water to a rolling boil and parboil the beans, in batches if necessary, removing them when they are still firm but not crunchy, 3 to 5 minutes. Set aside in a colander to cool.

About 3 minutes before serving time, heat about 2 tablespoons of the garlic-flavored oil in a large skillet and toss the beans in the oil to coat and reheat. Taste for seasoning. Garnish each serving with a few slices of browned garlic.

Daube of Beef

■ *Serves 6*

This is one of the easiest of beef stews: minimal cutting, no browning, just put everything together in the pot and bake. What gives it its Provençal flavor, in addition to the tomatoes and olive oil, is dried orange peel.

A key ingredient in an authentic Provençal daube de boeuf *is pork rind (skin). You won't likely find pork skin in your supermarket meat case, but ask the butcher (or better still, call ahead) if he can save you some. The additional fat the pork adds is removed before serving, as are the chunks of rind, leaving behind flavor and gelatin that give the sauce more body. If you can't find pork rind, a little bacon makes a stew that is less rich but still satisfying. In any case, this stew is best made a day or two ahead of time and refrigerated, which both improves the flavor and makes it easier to remove the fat. If possible, store the stew in a casserole that can go from the refrigerator to the oven to the table; follow the manufacturer's precautions about sudden changes of temperature.*

2½ pounds beef chuck steak or roast

1 teaspoon kosher salt

Freshly ground black pepper

1½ cups red wine

2 tablespoons olive oil

3 ounces sliced bacon, or 4 ounces fresh pork skin

1 medium onion, halved and sliced

1 cup sliced carrots

3 cloves garlic, chopped

5 ounces small mushrooms, whole or halved

2 cups peeled, chopped tomatoes (canned are fine), with juices

Bouquet garni of parsley, thyme, bay leaf, and dried orange peel (see Note)

Handful of niçoise or other black olives (optional)

1½ pounds egg noodles

WHICH BEER?

As with other "red wine" foods, a good hoppy pale ale or IPA.

Preheat the oven to 250°F. Separate the meat along the natural seams (see the Technique Note), remove the fat from the edges, and divide the larger muscles into pieces 2 to 3 inches square. If using a thicker roast, divide each piece across the grain to a thickness of ¾ to 1 inch. Season the meat generously with salt and pepper, and place it in a deep, covered casserole or Dutch oven. Add the wine and oil, toss to combine, and let stand while you prepare the rest of the ingredients.

If using bacon, quarter the slices and parboil the pieces for 2 minutes in a small pot of water. Drain and add to the casserole. If using pork skin, cut it into wide strips. Add the onions, carrots, garlic, mushrooms, and tomatoes to the casserole as you cut them up. Add the bouquet garni and the olives. Cover the casserole and bake until the meat is very tender, 3 to 4 hours. If time permits, transfer the stew to another container and refrigerate overnight. Remove the fat from the surface before reheating in a low oven. If serving the same day, let the stew rest for a while after baking and remove as much fat from the surface as you can.

Boil the noodles until tender, drain, place in a serving dish, and moisten with a cup or so of the stew juices. Discard the bouquet garni and correct the seasoning before serving the stew on or alongside the noodles.

NOTE There is no need to go out shopping for this; next time you eat an orange or tangerine (preferably organic or at least unsprayed), simply scrape the white pith off the inside of the pieces of peel, then let the strips dry on a sunny windowsill for a few days until leathery before storing them in a jar in the pantry.

NOTE I'm not trying to show off my fancy kitchen French, but bouquet garni is such a handy bit of shorthand for a basic item that every cook should know: a bundle of herbs (usually parsley, bay leaf, thyme, and sometimes celery and other ingredients, in this case orange peel), bound together with cotton twine so they can flavor a stew or sauce and then be fished out before serving.

TECHNIQUE NOTE My favorite cut for this kind of stew is whole blade or 7-bone chuck steaks. This large crosscut of the whole chuck (shoulder) naturally breaks down into three sections: the nearly round "eye," which is an extension of the central muscle of a rib roast and may have a rib bone attached; the rectangular "under blade" muscle, coarsest in texture; and two separate muscles on the other side of the shoulder blade bone, the "flatiron" and the "mock tender." The relative size of each of these three sections varies from one end of the chuck to the other. Where the blade bone is long and straight, the flatiron and rib eye are relatively large and there is almost no mock tender; at the other end, where the blade bone is shorter with a definite T or 7 shape, the mock tender is larger and the flatiron and rib eye almost disappear.

Breaking down a chuck steak (or, if it is cut thicker, a roast) is a simple matter of separating the muscles along their natural seams and trimming them of excess fat. If you find them at a good price, consider buying several and breaking them down, then sorting the cuts and freezing some for other uses. The flatiron makes a nice steak for grilling or pan-searing, although it does have a small seam of gristle down the middle; sliced across the grain, it's also ideal for stir-frying. The rib eye is tender enough to use as a steak as well. The mock tender, despite its name, is not very tender, and is best for moist heat along with the under blade and all the miscellaneous bits.

If all this seems too complicated, just buy one steak and use it all for your daube, chili, or whatever; some bites will come out more tender than others, but there's nothing wrong with that. Or you could simply pay the butcher to do the cutting and buy cubes of stewing beef.

Arroz con Pollo

▪ *Serves 6*

The typical Spanish method of cooking rice, used for the many varieties of paella as well as for this more prosaic chicken and rice dish, is in a shallow pan that maximizes the exposure of the rice grains to flavorful stock and spices. A short-grain Spanish rice such as Valencia will give the most authentic flavor and texture, but the more widely available Italian arborio will also give good results.

1/4 cup olive oil

6 chicken legs, divided into thighs and drumsticks

Kosher salt and freshly ground black pepper

1 medium onion, diced

3 cloves garlic, minced

1 pound tomatoes, peeled, seeded, and chopped

2 red or green peppers, roasted, peeled, and diced

1 pound green beans, trimmed and cut into 1-inch lengths

Leaves from 2 sprigs thyme

1/2 teaspoon saffron threads

2 cups Spanish or Italian short-grain rice

6 to 8 cups hot unsalted chicken stock

1 1/2 teaspoons kosher salt

WHICH BEER?

Pale ale or Pilsner

Heat the oil in a metal paella pan or flameproof earthenware *cazuela* over medium heat. Season the chicken with salt and pepper and cook it in the oil until golden. Remove and set aside. Add the onion and garlic and sauté until the onion begins to color. Add the tomatoes, peppers, beans, and thyme and cook 10 minutes. Preheat the oven to 350°F.

Crumble in the saffron, then stir in the rice, coating it well with the oil. Add the hot stock and salt, bring to a boil, and cook, stirring occasionally, until the rice begins to swell and absorb the liquid, 7 to 10 minutes. Arrange the chicken pieces on top of the rice and bake uncovered for 15 minutes, or until the rice has nearly absorbed the liquid. Remove from the oven, cover with a kitchen towel, and let stand 10 minutes.

Wild Mushroom Risotto

■ *Serves 4 as a first course or side dish, 2 as an entrée*

In an Italian meal, risotto is generally served on its own as a first course, like pasta or soup. Less commonly, it is served alongside simply cooked meats, like the Rosemary-Crusted Rack of Lamb on page 78. But I sometimes make a well-flavored risotto the main dish, preceded or followed by a salad.

8 ounces or more wild mushrooms—chanterelles, black chanterelles, hedgehogs, morels, or porcini

About 4 cups unsalted chicken stock

2 tablespoons olive oil

¼ cup finely chopped onion

1⅓ cups arborio rice

½ teaspoon kosher salt

Freshly ground black pepper

¼ cup grated Parmesan

WHICH BEER?
Pale or amber ale, or an ale in the Belgian "Abbey" style.

Brush away any dirt and debris from the mushrooms; wash them only if necessary. Discard any soggy or mushy parts, and inspect thick-stemmed varieties well for tiny worms. Cut the mushrooms into bite-size pieces according to their shape: chanterelles and porcini lengthwise through the stems and caps, morels left whole if small and halved lengthwise if larger.

Have the stock at a simmer in a saucepan. Heat the oil in a medium-sized heavy saucepan or deep skillet and sauté the onion and mushroom pieces just until the onion is translucent. (If using morels, black chanterelles, or other delicately textured mushrooms, remove them from the pan at this point and add them back to the risotto for the last few minutes of cooking.) Stir in the rice and cook for a minute or two, coating it thoroughly with the oil. Add enough stock to cover the rice. Stir in the salt and cook uncovered, stirring frequently, until the liquid is nearly absorbed. Continue adding stock a ladleful at a time, cooking until it is absorbed before the next addition. When the grains begin to swell, add the stock in smaller amounts, tasting a grain now and then to monitor the cooking rate. The goal is to finish with a loose, creamy mass of rice, with the center of each grain still firm. Check the seasoning, adding pepper to taste, stir in the cheese, and serve immediately.

VARIATION

Wild Mushroom Risotto II
(with Dried Mushrooms)

Soak 1 to 2 ounces dried porcini or other dried mushrooms in warm water to cover for at least 30 minutes prior to starting the risotto. Lift the soaked mushrooms out of the water and cut into bite-size pieces; proceed as in the main recipe, adding the soaked mushrooms when the onions begin to soften. Carefully decant or strain the soaking liquid and add it to the risotto with one of the early additions of stock.

Summer Vegetable "Napoleon"

■ *Serves 6 to 8*

This dish, a sort of layered ratatouille, is more properly called a terrine, but the term "napoleon" (a dessert of layers of puff pastry around a custard filling) has spilled over to the savory side of many restaurant menus to cover all sorts of dishes made up of many layers. Maybe it's because mille-feuille *("thousand leaves") is too hard to pronounce.*

Whatever you call it, this is an attractive way to present an assortment of peak summer vegetables. Try it warm from the oven, tepid, or at room temperature. It goes particularly well with grilled or poached salmon, either plain or with the roasted tomatillo sauce on page 181.

3 medium red bell peppers, roasted and peeled

2 small eggplants (about 1 pound in all)

1$\frac{1}{2}$ teaspoons kosher salt

$\frac{1}{4}$ teaspoon freshly ground pepper

8 ounces Ronde de Nice or other pale green summer squash

8 ounces green zucchini

8 ounces golden zucchini or yellow sunburst squash

2 tablespoons extra virgin olive oil

WHICH BEER?
Just about any, depending on
the main dish.

Preheat the oven to 400°F. If you have not already roasted the peppers, quarter them and lay them on a rimmed baking sheet to roast as the oven warms up (allow an extra half hour in this case).

Peel the eggplants and slice them crosswise about ⅛ inch thick. Cut the slices in half and sprinkle with salt and pepper. Cut the squashes to the same thickness, and keep in separate piles.

Lightly oil a 9- by 5-inch loaf pan. Arrange a fifth of the eggplant slices in a layer to cover the bottom of the pan completely. Top with a layer of the light green squash, seasoned with a little salt and pepper, then another layer of eggplant. Alternate eggplant layers with the red pepper, yellow squash, and zucchini, seasoning each layer as you go and finishing with a layer of eggplant. Drizzle the oil all over the top and bake uncovered until the terrine shrinks by about a quarter and pulls away from the sides of the pan, about 35 minutes. Remove from the oven and let cool slightly. To serve, invert a platter over the pan and turn the whole thing over, then remove the pan. Slice it in a Z pattern into wedges, and serve drizzled with any juices from the pan.

TECHNIQUE NOTE A mandoline (including the inexpensive plastic type) is the perfect tool for cutting the vegetables into even slices. Do not trim off the stems of the vegetables, as they make good handles to keep your fingertips away from the slicing blade. You can also use a food processor with a 4-millimeter slicing disk, although the machine tends to slice at random angles unless the food fits perfectly in the feed chute.

Penne with Broccoli, Garlic, and Bread Crumbs

■ *Serves 4*

They say broccoli is America's favorite fresh vegetable. I know my family is doing its share of the consumption, as we have this pasta dish at least once a week, with whatever seasonal beer we happen to be drinking.

1 pound broccoli crowns

1 pound short, tubular pasta, such as penne, penne rigate, mostaccioli, or rigatoni

¼ cup olive oil

⅓ cup dried bread crumbs (not too fine)

1 tablespoon minced garlic

¼ teaspoon red pepper flakes (optional)

½ cup grated Pecorino Romano

WHICH BEER?

Any.

Trim off any discolored base of the broccoli stems. Slice the stems crosswise about ⅛ inch thick, letting the florets fall away as you go, until the whole crown is reduced to bite-size pieces. Include any small, tender leaves.

Bring a pot of salted water to a boil (a pasta pot with a removable drainer is ideal). Add the broccoli stem pieces and cook 1 minute, then add the florets and cook until just tender, about 5 minutes. Remove with a slotted spoon or skimmer and drain.

Bring the water back to a boil and add the pasta. While the pasta cooks, warm a tablespoon or so of the olive oil in a large, deep skillet over low heat. Add the bread crumbs and cook, stirring, until the crumbs are golden brown. Add a few more drops of oil during cooking if the crumbs seem too dry. Scrape the crumbs out of the pan and set aside.

Return the skillet to the heat and add the remaining oil, garlic, and pepper flakes. Cook until fragrant, then stir in the broccoli. Toss to coat with the oil as the broccoli reheats, and taste for seasoning, bearing in mind the salt in the cheese. Remove from the heat if the broccoli is in danger of scorching before the pasta is done.

Drain the cooked pasta and add it to the broccoli mixture. Cook over high heat for a minute or so to evaporate any water clinging to the pasta, then stir in the bread crumbs and cheese and serve immediately.

VARIATION For a more pervasive garlic flavor, slice the garlic thinly and brown it slowly in the oil, as in Green Beans with Garlic Oil (page 79). Scatter the browned garlic slices on top just before serving.

Pasta with Sausage and Ricotta "Cream" Sauce

■ *Serves 6 as a first course, 3 to 4 as an entrée*

I had finally sworn off the "Alfredo" style of pasta sauces—those undeniably smooth and delicious cream reductions that are so loaded with butterfat that I now cringe at the thought of how many I ate when I was younger—when I came across this technique in Carlo Middione's book The Food of Southern Italy. *What a revelation it turned out to be! With the help of a little of the pasta cooking water and a lot of whisking, a big spoonful of ricotta produces a delicious sauce base with a much more reasonable level of fat. No, it's not as smooth as an Alfredo sauce, but it's still very satisfying. Here's a basic version adapted from Carlo's recipe, followed by one of my improvisations.*

8 ounces uncooked Italian sausage, sweet or hot according to your taste

1 pound short, tubular dried pasta, such as penne, mostaccioli, or cavatappi, or 1¼ pounds fresh fettuccine

12 ounces low-fat or whole-milk ricotta, the best you can find

Kosher salt, if necessary

⅓ cup grated Parmesan or aged Asiago

WHICH BEER?

Märzen or amber ale

Bring a large pot of salted water to a boil. Meanwhile, slit open the sausage casings and crumble the sausage into a medium skillet. Cook until nicely browned; drain on absorbent paper and keep warm. Warm a large mixing bowl (preferably one that can go straight to the table) with hot tap water, add the ricotta to the empty bowl, and place the bowl near the pasta pot.

When the water reaches a rolling boil, add the pasta, stirring as it returns to the boil. Cook according to the package directions, timing from the time the water returns to the boil and checking a minute or two ahead of the scheduled time. Halfway through cooking, ladle about a cup of water from the top of the pot into the bowl with the ricotta and beat it like crazy with a wire whisk. The texture should be like lightly whipped cream; if it's too thick, whisk in a little more pasta water. Taste for salt and correct if necessary, allowing for the salt in the sausage and cheese.

Drain the cooked pasta, add it to the bowl along with the sausage, and combine. Top with a little of the grated cheese and pass the rest of the cheese at the table.

VARIATIONS In place of the sausage, try one of the following:

■ Dried tomato: Reconstitute 6 sun-dried tomato halves in hot water, drain, and cut into julienne. Toss with the pasta and sauce.

■ Pesto: Use only 8 ounces of ricotta and stir in ⅓ to ½ cup pesto (recipe follows) just before adding the pasta.

■ Ham and peas: Sauté 3 or 4 sliced green onions and 1½ cups petite peas (blanched fresh or thawed frozen) in a little butter until heated through, then add to the bowl with 5 ounces finely diced Black Forest or similar ham.

Pesto

■ *Makes about 1 cup*

This Genovese basil sauce no longer needs an introduction, though today you are as likely to see it on pizza as on pasta. Store any extra tightly sealed in the refrigerator, and use within a week.

2 or 3 cloves garlic, peeled

Kosher salt

3 tablespoons pine nuts

Heaping cup basil leaves

½ cup grated Parmesan cheese, or half Parmesan and half Pecorino Romano

About ½ cup olive oil

To prepare the pesto in a food processor, combine everything but the oil and process to a rough paste, then add the oil with the motor running and process until smooth. Correct the seasoning.

To make the pesto by hand: Pound the garlic in a mortar with a generous pinch of salt. As the garlic breaks down, gradually add the pine nuts, then the basil, torn into small pieces. Continue pounding until everything is reduced to a paste, then stir in the cheese and oil to taste. Correct the seasoning.

FROM THE SPICE BAZAAR:

*Beer and the Foods of North Africa, the
Middle East, and India*

Thousands of years of spice trading have infused the foods of South
Asia and the Arab-influenced world with the aromas of coriander,
cumin, ginger, cinnamon, and countless other spices, plus dried fruits
and citrus. While the Muslim inhabitants of this region are forbidden to
drink any alcoholic beverages, the rest of us can enjoy these flavors with
a variety of beers.

Because of the tradition of hospitality in this part of the world, many
of the best-known foods of the Middle East and North Africa are
smaller dishes suitable for entertaining. The Levantine Dinner menu
on page 100 begins with an assortment of the tempting little dishes
called mezze, which also make great party fare. In the same spirit, offer
a variety of beers to suit everyone's taste. This is especially true with the
complex spices of an Indian curry or a Moroccan tajine; some guests
may prefer a beer that adds its own complexity of flavors, others might
want one that simply balances and refreshes.

Pantry Notes: North Africa to India

SPICES: Wherever there is a substantial South Asian or Middle Eastern
population, there are bound to be stores selling ingredients from home,
and these markets are likely to have the best selection and prices in
town on a whole range of spices, not just those used in their own local
cuisine. Try to buy whole spices whenever possible, especially ones you

can easily grind yourself, like peppercorns, cumin, coriander, cardamom, and cloves, not to mention small dried chiles, which are equally useful in East Asian and Latin American cooking. However, you may want to buy some preground spice blends like garam masala and curry powder; the latter may not be very authentic, but at least the version you buy in an Indian market is going to be better, fresher, and cheaper than anything at the supermarket.

BASMATI RICE: This long-grain rice with especially fine grains and a subtle, nutty aroma is preferred by most South Asians and also makes good Persian-style pilafs. Again, an Indian or Pakistani market will beat any other source of basmati in terms of price, selection, and quality.

Summertime and the Sippin' Is Easy: Pale Lagers

■

For all the inroads made by the micros, the vast majority of beer sold in North America is still of the same variety: pale, crystal-clear "premium" lagers like Budweiser, Coors, and Miller, pale imitations of the classic Pilsner style. Light in body, sweetish and soft, effervescent, and easy on the hop bitterness, these beers offer simple thirst-quenching refreshment on a hot day—what the craft-brew set calls "lawnmower beer." It's easy to get snobby about these beers, but sometimes they hit the spot better than a more "serious" beer, especially in hot weather or with very spicy food.

While some craft brewers have reacted to the dominance of the big national lagers by brewing dramatically different styles, others have chosen to compete directly with them on a quality level, brewing serious lagers in the Bohemian mold with all barley malt (no corn, rice, or other adjuncts that the big guys use to cut costs) and noble hops. Lager specialists like Gordon Biersch, Sudwerk, and Thomas Kemper make the best-known examples, while some mainly ale brewers like New Belgium and Lagunitas include good Pilsners in their line. Given the cost of ingredients and the brewing scale, however, these craft-brewed lagers can never really compete with mass-market domestic beers in price; rather, they take some market share away from European imports.

Even among the mass-market lagers, not all brands are the same; my personal favorite, Henry Weinhard's Private Reserve, has more hop flavor and aroma than most. And Samuel Adams Boston Lager (brewed for the West Coast market by Blitz-Weinhard), while hardly a microbrew and rather dark for a Pilsner, still sets the standard for what large American brewers can do in the Pilsner style if they choose to.

So when the food or the weather is really hot, or you just feel like a lighter and more refreshing brew, don't ignore the paler lagers. Just think quality over quantity, and support your local or regional brewers whenever you can.

Pappadams with Green Chutney

■ *Serves 8 as an appetizer*

Pappadams are thin, crisp, round wafers made from lentils and other legumes, often served in Indian restaurants as a complimentary nibble, much like the tortilla chips and salsa in Mexican places. I find them irresistible, with or without other Indian foods, and I always keep a package or two in my pantry, ready to toast.

Look for uncooked pappadams (or simply papad, among other spellings) in Indian markets as flat packages of twenty or so thin, leathery rounds. They come plain or in various flavors, including black pepper, garlic, and red chile, and will keep for months at room temperature. When heated, they expand by about 20 percent in size and become crisp. Most restaurants fry their pappadams, but they are just as good cooked by dry heat, either under a broiler or, easiest and fastest of all, one at a time over direct heat.

1 bunch cilantro

1 small green chile (serrano or jalapeño), seeds and
  ribs removed

1 green onion, sliced

1-inch chunk fresh ginger, peeled and sliced
  (to yield about 1 tablespoon minced)

2 tablespoons grated coconut, fresh or dried (optional)

$\frac{1}{2}$ teaspoon ground cumin

Pinch of kosher salt

$\frac{1}{2}$ cup unflavored yogurt

1 package pappadams (dried Indian lentil wafers)
  plain or spiced

Lemon juice

Wash the cilantro, and pull off enough leaves and smaller stems to make 2 cups. Drain briefly (it's fine if they are still wet) and combine in a blender or food processor with the chile, green onion, ginger, coconut, cumin, salt, and yogurt. Blend to a purée and set aside.

Toast the pappadams one at a time, directly over the burner on a gas stove or with an *asador* or other rack to hold them a little above an electric burner, until they expand and get noticeably lighter in color; turn repeatedly and move them around the heat so they cook evenly without scorching. Each one will take about 10 seconds. Transfer the cooked pappadams to a serving tray or basket.

Taste the chutney on a piece of pappadam and adjust the seasoning with lemon juice and more salt if needed (some pappadams are pretty salty by themselves). Transfer the chutney to small bowls for dipping.

WHICH BEER?

Any lager.

Kofta Kebab
(Minced Lamb on Skewers)

■ *Serves 4*

Shish kebab, cubes of marinated lamb grilled on skewers, may be the Middle Eastern meat dish most familiar to Americans, but I have a feeling the ground meat equivalent is more common in its native region. Cuisines all along the spice route have a tradition of molding meatball-like kofta mixtures of seasoned ground lamb onto metal skewers for grilling. Of course, the same mixture also makes tasty meatballs for cooking without the skewers.

1 medium onion

2 cloves garlic, peeled

3 or 4 sprigs cilantro

3 or 4 sprigs parsley

1$\frac{1}{2}$ pounds lamb shoulder

1 teaspoon kosher salt

1 teaspoon ground ginger

$\frac{1}{2}$ teaspoon ground cumin

$\frac{1}{4}$ teaspoon ground cinnamon

Pinch of cayenne or red pepper flakes (optional)

$\frac{1}{4}$ teaspoon freshly ground black pepper, or to taste

OPTIONAL ACCOMPANIMENTS

Pita, Naan (page 114), or similar soft flatbread

Diced and drained tomato

Plain yogurt, or yogurt mixed with diced and lightly salted cucumber

WHICH BEER?

Your favorite lager, or not-too-bitter ale.

Combine the onion, garlic, cilantro, and parsley in a food processor and chop finely. Separate the meat along the natural seams, discarding any large chunks of fat, and cut the meat into 1-inch pieces. Include any marrow from the arm bone if using shoulder chops. Add the meat, salt, and spices to the processor and process until the meat is finely chopped, the mixture forms a ball around the blade, and the fat smears the sides of the bowl. Check the seasoning (cook a bit in a skillet if you don't want to taste it raw) and adjust as needed.

With hands dipped in cold water, form the meat into 12 small cylinders, each molded around a short skewer. Pack the meat firmly onto the skewers to prevent its falling apart on the grill. Chill the skewered meat until about 15 minutes before grilling.

Light a moderate to hot fire in the grill. Grill the kebabs to the desired degree of doneness, about 7 minutes for medium-rare. Try to leave the meat in place on the grill for at least 4 to 5 minutes; if moved too soon, it is likely to stick or come apart. Serve on the skewers, sliding the meat off onto plates or onto soft pita or Indian-style bread, to top with tomatoes and yogurt.

Menu:
A Levantine Dinner for Eight

■

Dolmas

Baba Ghanoush

Hummus

Pea Soup Avgolemono

Pomegranate Chicken

Rice Pilaf with Almonds

■

Sudwerk Pilsner, Full Sail Amber Ale

This menu combines some of the favorite dishes of the lands of the eastern end of the Mediterranean. While religion prevents many residents of the region from drinking beer, their cuisines still provide us with lots of beer-friendly foods; not surprising, since this is where humans first cultivated grains thousands of years ago, and first converted them into something we would recognize as beer .

Dolmas *(Stuffed Grape Leaves)*

▓ *Makes about 3 dozen*

This is only one possible filling for dolmas; raisins or currants, nuts, and other vegetables are all popular additions. If you have some leftover cooked lamb or beef, they work fine in a dolmas stuffing. So do uncooked trimmings, minced by hand or chopped in a food processor or meat grinder. Since this is part of a menu that uses a lot of chicken stock, making your own stock from reserved bones and giblets should provide plenty of material (gizzards, hearts, and meat gleaned from neck and backs) to include in the dolmas. I would also include the liver and heart from the Pomegranate Chicken (page 106).

Dolmas can be made several days in advance and refrigerated; remove them from the refrigerator a couple of hours ahead of time to serve cool, or reheat them gently with a little more water if you like them warm.

$3/4$ **cup minced cooked roast beef or lamb or cooked chicken giblets, or 10 ounces ground lamb or beef**

1 chicken liver and heart

2 tablespoons olive oil

$1/4$ **cup minced onion**

2 tablespoons minced garlic

2 tablespoons minced parsley, cilantro, or a blend

$3/4$ **teaspoon ground cumin**

$3/4$ **teaspoon ground coriander**

$1/4$ **teaspoon ground cinnamon**

$1/4$ **teaspoon freshly ground pepper, or to taste**

3 cups cooked rice, cooled

$1/4$ **teaspoon kosher salt, or to taste**

1 jar (8 ounces) grape leaves

2 tablespoons lemon juice

If using raw meat, cook it in a skillet with the chicken liver and heart until the ground meat is crumbly and lightly browned and the giblets are no longer pink inside. If using cooked meat, start the liver and heart cooking first, and add the minced meat only if you need to cook out some fat. Transfer the browned meats to a sieve set over a heatproof container to drain. Pull out the liver and heart and chop finely by hand.

Add 1 tablespoon of the oil to the skillet and cook the onion over medium heat until soft but not browned. Add the garlic and chopped herbs and cook until fragrant. Add the chopped meats and spices and cook for another minute or so. Scrape the contents of the skillet over the rice in a bowl and mix thoroughly. Check the meat drippings; if there is enough liquid underneath the fat to bother with, draw it out with a bulb baster and add it to the rice mixture. Add salt to taste.

Preheat the oven to 350°F. Carefully work the roll of grape leaves out of the jar, working over a bowl to catch the brine if you expect to have any leaves left over. Rinse the leaves in a large bowl of water and drain.

Lay a leaf out on a work surface with the stem nearest you, facing up. Cut off the stem with scissors or a paring knife. Place a level tablespoon of the filling near the stem end. Fold the two nearest points of the leaf over the filling, then fold in the sides, and roll into a firm cylinder about 2 inches long. Place seam down in a 9- by 13-inch baking dish. Repeat with the remaining leaves and filling, packing the rolls snugly in the dish. Store any leftover leaves in the original brine, and plan to use them within a week or so.

Add water to the pan to halfway cover the dolmas. Drizzle with the lemon juice and the remaining tablespoon of oil. Cover the pan tightly with foil and bake until the liquid is nearly gone and the leaves are quite tender, 35 to 40 minutes.

Baba Ghanoush *(Roasted Eggplant Dip)*

■ *Serves 8 as an appetizer*

Even people who don't like eggplant seem to go for this smooth, rich-tasting eggplant purée, as a dip for pita wedges or inner leaves of romaine.

1 pound eggplant

1 medium onion

2 tablespoons olive oil

1 large clove garlic, minced

1 tablespoon sesame tahini

2 tablespoons lemon juice

$1/2$ teaspoon kosher salt, or to taste

Freshly ground white pepper or cayenne to taste

6 to 8 pita breads or smaller leaves from 2 romaine hearts (for both this and the Hummus)

Puncture the eggplant skin in a few places and roast in a shallow pan with the onion in a 400°F oven until the eggplant is thoroughly soft. Remove and set aside until cool enough to handle. (This can be done a day or two ahead and refrigerated.)

Split the eggplant lengthwise and carefully scrape all the flesh away from the skin. Discard the skin and chop the flesh finely. Split the onion, discard the skin and any burnt parts, and chop finely.

Combine the oil and garlic in a large skillet and heat until fragrant. Add the chopped onion and cook 2 minutes, adjusting the heat so the garlic does not brown. Remove the pan from the heat. Stir in the tahini, lemon juice, and eggplant and season to taste with salt and white pepper. If you want a smoother texture, transfer the mixture to a food processor and process to a chunky purée. Serve at room temperature with pita wedges or romaine leaves.

Hummus

■ *Makes 2 cups*

Keep a can of chickpeas (garbanzo beans), a jar of tahini, and some lemon juice on hand and you can always whip up a batch of hummus. If your friends and family are like mine, it will always be one of the first things to disappear.

1 can (15 ounces) garbanzo beans

3 tablespoons sesame tahini

2 cloves garlic, peeled

1 teaspoon kosher salt, or to taste

$\frac{1}{4}$ teaspoon paprika, sweet or hot

$\frac{1}{4}$ cup lemon juice, or to taste

Drain the beans, saving the broth. Combine with the remaining ingredients in a food processor or blender and blend to a smooth paste, thinning with as much of the bean broth as needed to make a thick but scoopable paste. Let stand for at least an hour for the flavors to blend, and check the seasoning before serving. Use as a dip with pita or romaine leaves.

Pea Soup Avgolemono

■ *Serves 8*

This is not what we usually think of as pea soup; instead, it's a light broth with whole peas finished with the lemon and egg yolk mixture known in Greek cuisine as avgolemono. When you can get really fresh, tender peas in the pod, by all means use them; the rest of the time, use frozen petite peas, which are definitely worth the price premium over the bigger, starchier ones just labeled "peas."

Other bright green seasonal vegetables will also work, visually as well as in terms of flavor: Try blanched and peeled fava beans, sliced asparagus, baby spinach, or quarter or half slices of slender zucchini.

8 cups chicken stock, preferably homemade

Kosher salt and freshly ground black pepper

3 eggs

¼ cup fresh lemon juice

1½ cups fresh or frozen petite peas

Bring the stock to a simmer and season to taste with salt and pepper. Meanwhile, beat the eggs and lemon juice together in a medium bowl. Add the peas to the stock and cook just until tender (frozen peas are already tender and just need to be heated through). Reduce the heat so the soup barely simmers; you do not want to boil it once you add the egg.

Ladle a cup or so of broth into the bowl with the eggs and whisk to combine, then pour the mixture into the soup. The egg will cook in a few seconds, thickening the soup slightly. Ladle the soup into cups or bowls and serve immediately.

Pomegranate Chicken

▨ *Serves 8*

This recipe will work with cut-up whole fryers or your favorite chicken parts. The key ingredient here is pomegranate concentrate, sometimes called pomegranate molasses, which is simply the juice from fresh pomegranate seeds reduced to a syrup. It's sold in bottles in Middle Eastern groceries.

2 small frying chickens, 3 to 3½ pounds each, or the equivalent in chicken parts

Kosher salt

1 teaspoon freshly ground pepper

3 tablespoons pomegranate concentrate

Cut whole chickens into quarters, or break them down further into breast halves, wings, drumsticks, and thighs. Save the backs, necks, and giblets for stock. Trim off any excess skin and fat.

If seasoning the chicken, sprinkle it lightly with salt (about 1 teaspoon per chicken) and pepper; cover and refrigerate. If starting within a few hours of cooking, use two or three times as much salt, most of which will rinse away.

Preheat the oven to 350°F. Rinse the chicken and pat dry. Choose a baking dish that will fit all the pieces in one layer, not too snugly; if this is impossible, use one dish for legs, another for breasts and wings. Rub the chicken pieces with 2 tablespoons of the pomegranate concentrate and arrange them skin side up in the pans. Bake uncovered 30 minutes, brush with the remaining 1 tablespoon of concentrate, and bake another 15 minutes, or until the juices run clear and the breast and thigh meat register 160°F on an instant-read thermometer.

Rice Pilaf with Almonds

■ *Serves 8*

Pilaf is a method of cooking rice (and sometimes other grains) that begins with cooking the dry grains in oil, then adding the liquid all at once and cooking the rice undisturbed. Pilafs can be main dishes containing meats and vegetables, or side dishes like this.

2 cups long-grain white rice, preferably basmati or jasmine

2 tablespoons olive oil

1/2 cup slivered almonds

1/2 cup minced onion

3 1/2 cups unsalted chicken stock, or half stock and half water

1 teaspoon kosher salt

Soak the rice in cold water for 30 minutes and drain thoroughly. Warm the oil in a 10-inch or larger skillet and add the almonds. Cook over low heat, stirring constantly, until the almonds are lightly browned. Remove the almonds with a slotted spoon and set aside. Add the onions to the pan and cook until they are soft and beginning to color, but not browned. Add the rice, stir to coat with the oil, and cook for a minute or two. Add the stock and salt, bring just to a boil, and reduce the heat as low as possible. Cover and cook until all of the liquid is absorbed, about 20 minutes. Stir in the almonds, replace the cover, and let stand for 5 minutes before serving.

VARIATIONS Pilafs lend themselves to lots of variations; just try to avoid too much repetition of ingredients from other dishes in the menu. Here are some possibilities:

■ Crumble a large pinch of saffron threads into a small bowl of stock and set in a warm place while soaking the rice. Add the mixture along with the rest of the stock.

■ Add a handful of raisins, dried currants, or diced dried apricots (plumped in a little warm water) to the pilaf at the end, with the almonds.

■ Substitute chopped pistachios (skip the initial frying step) or raw cashews (which definitely need frying) for the almonds.

Lamb and Vegetable Tajine with Chickpea Couscous

■ *Serves 8*

In a Moroccan banquet, the couscous comes last, with its own accompaniment of broth, vegetables, and meat, and there is often another fragrant stew (called a tajine) served earlier in the meal. In this more casual, family-style menu, the two are combined, with the broth from the tajine used to moisten the couscous, and the vegetables and lamb heaped on top.

A couple of lamb shanks split eight ways is not a lot of meat, but that's just the point. This is mostly a dish of grain and vegetables, with a rich, spicy lamb broth accented by a few bits of meat. Feel free to add more lamb (cubes of shoulder meat work well) if you want a meatier dish.

I've adapted this from a recipe by Mohamed Ben Mchabcheb (L'Olive restaurant, Chicago) in Fine Cooking, *March 2000. Don't be alarmed by the number of ingredients and steps; much of the vegetable prep work can be done while the broth simmers and the couscous alternately steams and rests.*

WHICH BEER?

Amber or pale ale, Märzen.

BROTH

¼ cup olive oil

2 lamb shanks

Kosher salt and freshly ground black pepper

1 cup sliced onion

2 teaspoons ground ginger

2 teaspoons ground coriander

1 teaspoon paprika

½ teaspoon ground cinnamon

1 pound tomatoes, quartered

1 large red bell pepper, cut into large dice

8 to 10 sprigs each parsley and cilantro, tied together

1 bay leaf

Heaping teaspoon kosher salt

COUSCOUS

1 pound couscous

2 cups warm water

2 tablespoons olive oil

Large pinch of saffron threads

$1/4$ teaspoon turmeric

2 teaspoons kosher salt

Black or white pepper to taste

VEGETABLES AND FINAL ASSEMBLY

1 pound baby artichokes

1 pound carrots, peeled, split lengthwise if large, and cut
  into 1-inch sections

1 medium sweet potato, peeled and cut into 1-inch cubes

1 pound butternut squash, peeled, sliced across into 1-inch slabs,
  then cut into wedges

1 pound zucchini, halved or quartered lengthwise, cut across
  into 1-inch sections

1 small head cauliflower, cut into florets

1 can chickpeas, drained

$1/2$ cup raisins, soaked in a little warm water until plump

Harissa or Southeast Asian–style red chile and garlic paste

To make the broth, heat about half the oil in a large saucepan or stock-pot over medium heat. Season the lamb shanks with salt and pepper and start them browning in the oil. Meanwhile, toss the sliced onions with the ginger, coriander, paprika, cinnamon, and the remaining oil. When the shanks are well browned, push them aside and add the onion mixture. Cook, stirring frequently, until the spices are quite fragrant. Add the tomatoes, red pepper, herb bundle, bay leaf, salt, and water to cover by about 1 inch. Simmer until the meat is quite tender, $1\frac{1}{2}$ to 2 hours.

About an hour before serving time, spread the couscous in a large, shallow bowl (the bowl you will serve in is fine). Pour in enough cool water to barely cover the grains, then pour off as much water as possible, holding the grains back with your hand. Spread the grains out in an even layer and let stand 5 minutes. Meanwhile, combine the warm water, oil, and seasonings, and bring at least 2 inches of water to a boil in the bottom of a couscoussière or a pot with a metal colander fitted into the top. Moisten your hands with a little of the seasoned water and rub the soaked couscous between your hands to break up the clumps. Continue rubbing and moistening until the mixture is evenly crumbly, then gradually scatter it over the inside of the couscoussière. Cook uncovered until the couscous grains have swelled noticeably, 10 to 15 minutes.

Meanwhile, start preparing the vegetables: Remove the outer artichoke leaves until the leaves are more yellow than green. Slice off the top third of the artichoke and pare away any dark green parts on the stem end (but leave some stem attached). Split lengthwise, and if the chokes are developed, cut them out of each half with the tip of a knife or a melon scoop. Drop the prepared artichokes into a bowl of water acidulated with a little lemon juice or vinegar.

After the first steaming, carefully remove the top of the couscoussière and dump the steamed couscous out into the bowl. As soon as the couscous has cooled enough to handle, rub it again between your hands, adding more of the seasoned water. Repeat the steaming, cooling, and rubbing steps. Meanwhile, continue with the vegetable preparations.

When the lamb is tender, remove the shanks from the pot, discard the herb bundle, and skim as much fat as possible from the surface. Add the artichokes to the lamb broth 30 minutes before serving time. Add the carrots, sweet potato, and squash 10 minutes later, and return the couscous to the couscoussière for a final steaming. Add the zucchini and cauliflower for the last 10 minutes. Meanwhile, pull the lamb meat off the bones, cut it into bite-size pieces, and add them back to the broth. Check the broth for seasoning and adjust if needed.

Turn the steamed couscous out into the serving dish, and mix in the chickpeas and raisins. Shape it into a wide mound with a well in the center. Spoon the lamp and vegetable mixture into the center with a slotted spoon, and ladle some of the broth over the couscous. Pass additional broth at the table, some plain and some mixed with harissa.

Chicken Curry with Cashews

■ *Serves 4 to 6*

This is more or less based on the Moghul korma *style of rich, creamy curries from northern India, thickened and enriched with ground cashews. Feel free to make it hotter or milder by varying the proportion of sweet and hot paprika and cayenne. I like it best with chicken legs, but use breasts or other parts as you like. It also makes a great way to serve leftover roast turkey (see the variations).*

$^1/_4$ **teaspoon peppercorns**

$^1/_2$ **teaspoon cumin seeds**

$^1/_2$ **cinnamon stick, broken into small pieces**

5 cloves

5 cardamom pods

$^1/_2$ **teaspoon ground turmeric**

1 teaspoon hot paprika, or $^3/_4$ teaspoon sweet paprika plus $^1/_4$ teaspoon cayenne

3 tablespoons oil, or half oil and half butter

1$^1/_2$ cups finely diced onion

1 tablespoon minced garlic

1 tablespoon minced ginger

4 chicken legs

1 teaspoon kosher salt, or to taste

1 bay leaf

2 cups water

$^1/_4$ **cup raw cashews**

$^1/_2$ **cup plain whole-milk yogurt**

WHICH BEER?

Märzen or other dark lager.

Toast the whole spices in a dry pan (you might as well use the same one you will use to make the curry) until quite fragrant. Grind in a mortar or spice grinder (discard the cardamom husks and grind just the seeds). Combine with the turmeric and paprika and set aside.

Heat the oil in a wide saucepan over low heat. Add the onion, garlic, and ginger and cook slowly, stirring frequently, until the onion is just starting to turn golden; this may take 15 minutes. Meanwhile, skin the chicken legs and separate at the joints; if you like, you can hack each leg section through the bone Chinese style into 2 or 3 pieces. Season with a little of the salt.

Stir the spice mix and bay leaf into the onions and cook until fragrant. Push the onions to the side and add the chicken pieces to the middle, turning to coat them with the spice-stained oil. Add the water and remaining salt, bring to a simmer, and cook uncovered until the chicken is quite tender, about 45 minutes.

Grind the cashews in the mortar, or chop and mash with a knife (see Technique Note). When the chicken is tender, stir the cashew paste and yogurt into the sauce, correct the seasoning, and keep warm until ready to serve. Do not let the sauce boil after adding the yogurt or it may curdle.

Serve with rice, Naan (recipe follows), or both.

TECHNIQUE NOTE A lot of recipes for cashew-thickened curries call for grinding the nuts in a blender with some of the cooking liquid, but I find a mortar and pestle to work much better to reduce a handful of cashews to a paste. If you don't have a mortar and pestle, simply chop the nuts as finely as possible with a knife and then mash the chopped pieces against the cutting board with the side of the knife blade, using a kneading motion. Another option is to buy some cashew butter at the health food store.

NOTE If you don't feel like toasting and grinding your own spices, use 1 tablespoon commercial curry powder plus ½ teaspoon each sweet paprika and ground cinnamon and a pinch of ground cloves. Adjust the heat to taste with cayenne.

VARIATION

Leftover Turkey Curry

Along with turkey sandwiches and turkey slices warmed up in the last of the gravy, the post-Thanksgiving weekend in my family often includes a turkey curry.

Prepare the basic curry without the chicken; when the onions are quite soft and the sauce is full of flavor, add the cashews and yogurt, then add 2 to 3 cups of cubed roast turkey.

VARIATION

Vegetarian Korma

In place of the chicken, use 4 cups assorted diced vegetables such as winter squash, potatoes, sweet potatoes, carrots, and parsnips. Cut slower-cooking vegetables like white potatoes into somewhat smaller pieces than faster-cooking varieties, or add them to the pan sooner. Peas can be stirred in for just the last few minutes of cooking.

Naan (Tandoori-Style Flatbread)

▨ *Makes 8*

These tender flatbreads are typically baked right on the walls of the clay tandoor oven in an Indian restaurant, but you can make them on a griddle at home. The yeasted dough here is not typical, but it eliminates the long resting period in traditional recipes, allowing you to serve them within an hour after you begin.

$\frac{1}{2}$ **teaspoon active dry yeast**

$\frac{1}{3}$ **cup lukewarm water**

$\frac{1}{2}$ **cup milk**

1 tablespoon butter

About 2$\frac{1}{4}$ cups all-purpose flour

Scant teaspoon kosher salt

1 to 2 teaspoons oil

Melted butter or ghee, for brushing (optional)

In a small bowl, sprinkle the yeast over the water and let it stand until the yeast sinks. Warm the milk and butter in a small saucepan to about baby-bottle temperature; turn off the heat and let the mixture stand until the butter melts.

Put 2 cups flour and the salt in a food processor. With the motor running, add the milk mixture through the feed tube, then add the yeast mixture. Process until the mixture forms a dough that cleans the sides of the bowl; add a tablespoon or two of flour if needed. Turn the dough out onto a lightly floured surface and knead by hand for a minute or two until smooth and not too sticky. Oil a medium bowl, put the ball of dough in the bowl and turn to coat the dough with oil. Cover and let it stand 30 to 45 minutes. The dough may not double in size, but it should rise noticeably.

Punch down the dough and divide it into 8 pieces. Preheat a griddle or heavy skillet over medium heat. Gently stretch and roll a piece of dough out into a 7-inch circle and lay it on the griddle. (When you pick it up off the board, it will likely stretch a bit into an irregular oval, which is fine.) Cook on the griddle until the underside is well speckled with golden brown, about 1 minute; turn and continue baking until nicely browned on the second side, another minute or so. Continue with the remaining pieces of dough, transferring the naan to a platter or cloth-lined basket as they are done. Brush the hot breads with a little butter or ghee, if you like a richer, shinier bread. Serve immediately.

NOTE Leftover naan can be frozen; skip the final buttering, cool on a wire rack and then freeze on the same rack, transferring them to a plastic bag when frozen. Reheat on a griddle before serving.

VARIATION Naan are easily varied with herbs and spices. Try adding 2 tablespoons sliced green onions or dill or ½ teaspoon ground cumin to the dough before the final kneading.

Gobhi Bhaji
(Pan-Fried Cauliflower with Spices)

■ *Serves 4 to 6*

Although you would hardly know it from most restaurant menus, India has a whole genre of "dry" vegetable dishes cooked in a shallow pan without added liquid. This is a much slower cooking method than Chinese-style stir-frying, allowing more time for the spice-infused oil to seep into firm vegetables like cauliflower and potatoes. Try this along with other dishes in an Indian meal or as a side dish with a Western-style entrée.

1 head cauliflower (about 1¹⁄₂ pounds)

8 ounces fresh tomatoes

3 tablespoons oil

¹⁄₄ teaspoon cumin seeds

¹⁄₈ teaspoon mustard seeds

2 small whole dried chiles

¹⁄₂ teaspoon ground turmeric

¹⁄₄ cup minced onion or shallot

1 tablespoon minced fresh ginger

Heaping ¹⁄₂ teaspoon kosher salt, or to taste

WHICH BEER?

Pilsner or other pale lager.

Cut the cauliflower apart into large florets; discard the central stem. Slice across the stems of the florets until they fall apart into bite-size sections and tender stem slices. Set aside. Halve the tomatoes and grate the halves on a box grater into a bowl, grating down to and discarding the skins.

Combine the oil, cumin, mustard, and chiles in a wok or stir-fry pan and set over medium-low heat. Cook until the seeds begin to sizzle and pop. Sprinkle in the turmeric, then stir in the onion and ginger and cook until the onion softens. Add the cauliflower pieces, toss to coat with the spiced oil, and add the grated tomato and salt. Cook, stirring occasionally, until the cauliflower is tender, about 30 minutes. Adjust the seasoning and discard the chiles before serving.

Curried Winter Squash Soup

■ *Serves 8*

This isn't an Indian dish, just an example of how Indian spices have worked their way into the world's cooking. Something about the yellow-orange color of squash suggests the color of curry spices, and I have always liked the flavor combination too. This is one place where a standard packaged curry powder works fine; just make sure it's reasonably fresh. Add some hearty bread, a salad, and a rich-tasting ale and you have a good cold-weather supper.

3 tablespoons butter or oil

1 teaspoon curry powder

1 large onion, sliced

2 pounds winter squash such as butternut, acorn, kabocha, or Delicata

6 cups chicken or vegetable stock

Kosher salt and freshly ground black pepper

½ cup sour cream (regular or low-fat) or plain yogurt, lightly whipped

Chopped chives or parsley, for garnish

WHICH BEER?

Sweet stout or "winter warmer" ale.

Melt the butter in a soup pot over medium-low heat. Add the curry powder and cook until fragrant, about 1 minute. Add the onions, cover, and cook until soft, about 10 minutes. Meanwhile, peel and seed the squash (see the Technique Note) and cut it into ¾-inch chunks. Add to the pot with the stock and a few good pinches of salt. Bring to a boil, reduce the heat, and simmer until the squash is quite tender, about 40 minutes.

Purée the contents of the pot in a food processor or blender (do it in several batches to avoid spills), or put it through a food mill. (The soup can be made to this point ahead of time.)

Return the soup to the pot, season to taste, and simmer until reheated. Serve each portion topped with a dollop of sour cream or yogurt and garnished with chopped chives or parsley.

TECHNIQUE NOTE Peeling hard-shelled squash can be a bit of a nuisance, especially those with odd shapes like acorn or Delicata. If you have a food mill, you can skip the peeling step, as the mill strains out the skins as it purées the flesh. Otherwise, you might want to stick with butternut squash, the easiest variety to peel.

VARIATION For a fancier soup, you can add your choice of 1 pound raw shrimp or ¾ pound cooked shrimp, crab, or lobster meat. If using uncooked shrimp, peel and devein and cut into large dice, and cook it in the butter with just a pinch of the curry powder, then remove it with a slotted spoon and set aside in the refrigerator. Add the shellfish to the soup just before the final reheating.

7
MALT AND HOPS, MEET GINGER AND SOY:

Beer and the Foods of East and Southeast Asia

From the delicate steamed and simmered dishes of Japan to the earthy sesame and chile flavors of Korea to the huge variety of Chinese cooking, the subtle caramel-anchored dishes of Vietnam and the intricate chile and spice blends of Thailand and Indonesia, Asian cuisines offer enough flavors for a lifetime of exploration by the beer-loving cook. No wonder European-style brewing has found a foothold throughout East and Southeast Asia.

As a broad generalization, Asian cuisines do a better job than their Western counterparts of integrating the five primary flavors (sweet, sour, salty, bitter, and hot) in the food. As a result, they rely less on beverages like beer and wine to "complete" a meal. This can make certain matches tricky, especially with highly hopped beers. The bitter astringency that makes a dry-finishing pale ale so refreshing with European-style meat dishes can throw the whole balance of an Asian meal out of whack. It's no wonder, then, that the beers imported from the home country in most Asian restaurants tend to be bland, pale "international" style lagers; close your eyes and you could be drinking Bud (and probably should, since it will be cheaper and fresher). But we don't have to fall into the same trap at home. I look to amber and brown ales and Märzen and dunkel style lagers to bring a nice malty richness to the equation without overwhelming the food with hops.

Pantry Notes: East and Southeast Asia

Many of the Asian ingredients called for in this chapter are available in supermarkets, but wherever there is a significant Asian population you are likely to find specialty stores (and, increasingly, pan-Asian supermarkets) selling fresh, dried, and canned goods from many Asian countries. These are also likely to be the best sources in town for really fresh meats, seafood, and poultry. Here are some things to stock up on.

SOY SAUCE: Unless noted otherwise, the recipes in this chapter were developed with a standard "thin" soy sauce. I mainly use Pearl River Bridge Superior Thin Soy Sauce from China, but ordinary Kikkoman or Yamasa will also work fine.

FISH SAUCE: A thin, salty liquid extract of anchovies, used like soy sauce in mainland Southeast Asian cuisines. Most fish sauces come from Thailand, even when labeled in Vietnamese. The brands sold in glass bottles are generally much better than the plastic-bottle versions and are not much more expensive.

GINGER: Now available in most supermarkets, but the quality is usually better in Asian markets. The color and thickness of the skin varies with the season and source, but any time of year look for firm rhizomes with tight skin. Store ginger in the vegetable crisper, wrapped in a paper towel, replacing the paper each time you cut some and it will keep for weeks.

GALANGAL, GALANGA: A cousin of ginger with a mustardy, medicinal aroma, used in Thai cooking. Dry forms (slices, flakes, or powder) may be labeled "laos root" or simply "laos."

LEMONGRASS: An aromatic stalk like a stiff, waxy scallion, now cultivated in North America, lemongrass keeps for weeks in the refrigerator and also grows easily from stalks rooted in water.

CURRY PASTES, THAI: Purists still pound their own curry pastes out of chiles, garlic, onion, lemongrass, galangal, and spices, but very good commercial versions are sold in most Asian markets. Green pastes are generally the hottest, red pastes slightly less so. Mussulman (the spelling varies) pastes include an Indian-style blend of spices.

COCONUT MILK: Again, you can grate and squeeze fresh coconut, but with excellent canned coconut milk available from Thailand and Malaysia at less than a buck a can, why bother?

MUSHROOMS, BLACK: Widely known under the Japanese name shiitake. Good dried versions come from China, Japan, and Korea. Fresh shiitake are grown here and are widely available, but I'm not crazy about the flavor and generally prefer the dried ones.

SESAME OIL: A brown, deeply fragrant oil pressed from toasted sesame seeds, used in small quantities as a flavoring condiment in Chinese, Japanese, and especially Korean cuisines. Look for 100 percent sesame oil; some cheaper brands are blended with other oils and have less flavor. Do not confuse this oil with the lighter-colored cold-pressed sesame oils sold in health food stores.

At the Malt Shop: Amber, Red, and Brown Ales

▪

This category is admittedly a catchall for various "not too" styles, often occupying a middle ground in a brewer's line—copper-colored to reddish-brown ales that are darker than pale ale but lighter than porter. "Red" is less popular as a label term than it was a few years ago, but "amber" is still in wide use. A few examples are labeled "altbier" (or abbreviated "alt"), German for "old beer," old in this sense meaning old-fashioned ale brewing as opposed to the more modern lager.

As a group, these ales tend to emphasize malty flavors, sometimes finishing dry, sometimes noticeably sweet. The hop element is all over the map but tends to be higher in beers labeled "amber" and lower in those labeled "brown" (though the latter is still likely to be more bitter than an English brown ale). All in all, these are very agreeable beers that are often a better match for spicy foods than hoppier ales. But more than any other group, this is one where you have to get to know individual brands to find your favorites. Mine include Full Sail Amber Ale (on the hoppy side for an amber), Lost Coast Downtown Brown (a sweetish ale that goes nicely with spicy foods), Pete's Wicked Ale (a brown that is far milder than its name would suggest), New Belgium Abbey Belgian Style Ale, and Widmer Springfest (a seasonal altbier).

Red-Cooked ("Master Sauce") Chicken

■ *Serves 4 to 6*

I think Master Sauce Chicken was the first dish I ever made out of Barbara Tropp's 1982 cookbook The Modern Art of Chinese Cooking, *and I have made it hundreds of times since then (except for a couple of months during my wife's pregnancy when she inexplicably couldn't stand the smell of it). Fragrant with soy sauce, wine, and spices, with a beautiful mahogany sheen to the skin, it's simply one of the world's most delicious ways to serve chicken, hot or cold or anywhere in between. The "master sauce" refers to the rich soy sauce broth left over from cooking the bird, which can be used again and again—just replenish the seasonings—and gets better each time.*

Traditionalists insist on a Chinese clay pot for this kind of dish, but I have always used my 3¹/₂-quart Le Creuset Dutch oven, which is the perfect size for a robust 4-pound-plus Chinatown chicken.

2 cups water

2 cups soy sauce

¹/₂ cup Chinese rice wine or dry sherry

2 tablespoons sugar

4 or 5 slices ginger

2 green onions, halved and crushed

2 pods star anise and ¹/₂ cinnamon stick, or 1 teaspoon Chinese five-spice powder

1 strip dried orange peel (see page 81; optional)

1 whole chicken, 4 to 5 pounds

WHICH BEER?

Amber ale.

Combine the liquids and seasonings in a deep covered casserole (hold back some of the water if you are making the dish for the first time and are not sure of the capacity of your pot). Bring to a simmer. Meanwhile, remove the excess fat and the kidneys from the chicken, rinse well inside and out, and pat dry.

When the liquid is nearly boiling, carefully lower the chicken into the pot, breast side up. If the liquid does not cover the chicken, add more hot water (as much as you can without overflowing the pot). While the liquid comes back to a boil, ladle it over any exposed skin to provide even coloring. Reduce the heat to very low, cover the pot, and simmer 50 minutes to an hour, uncovering the pot a few times to baste the exposed skin with the sauce. For the best flavor, turn off the heat and let the chicken steep another half hour to 2 hours, basting occasionally.

To serve, either lift the chicken out of the pot with a spoon inserted in the cavity and another outside (be careful not to tear the skin) or pour off the sauce into a bowl. Carve the chicken Western style or chop it through the bone Chinese style, as you like. Serve warm, at room temperature, or cold.

Strain the sauce through a fine sieve and freeze it for the next time. Discard the fat before thawing and refresh the flavors each time you use it with ½ cup fresh soy sauce and half of the other flavoring ingredients.

VARIATION

Red-Cooked Pork

A pork shoulder roast, including the cut called Boston butt even though it comes from the shoulder, is also delicious red-cooked. You could use the same master sauce as the chicken, but I prefer to keep them separate and season them a little differently, replacing the star anise, cinnamon, and orange peel with 1 teaspoon Sichuan peppercorns. Leftovers will keep for the better part of a week in the refrigerator and are good as a last-minute addition to vegetable stir-fry dishes, noodle dishes, or fried rice.

Wok-Smoked Chicken

■ *Serves 4 to 6*

Stovetop smoking in a wok can be the sole method of cooking smaller pieces of meat, like the Hunan-style pork on page 128, but larger pieces like a whole chicken generally need a preliminary cooking by some other method, with the smoking mainly as a flavor step. Smoked chicken is delicious warm from the smoker, but it's also useful days later in salads such as the one on page 192 or as cold picnic food.

1 tablespoon Sichuan peppercorns

2 tablespoons kosher salt

1 whole chicken, trimmed of excess fat, or 3 to 4 pounds chicken parts

2 green onions, trimmed and halved

3 slices ginger

1 pod star anise

¼ cup tea leaves

¼ cup raw rice

¼ cup sugar

1 cinnamon stick, crumbled

WHICH BEER?

Amber or pale ale.

Toast the Sichuan peppercorns in a dry skillet until fragrant. Grind to a powder in a mortar or spice grinder and combine with the salt. Rinse the chicken and pat dry. Rub the salt mixture all over the chicken, inside and out. Marinate 8 hours to overnight in the refrigerator.

To steam the chicken, you will need a wok, covered roaster, or other large covered pan with a rack that will hold the chicken in a deep plate or glass pie pan an inch or so above boiling water. Drain the chicken, put the green onion, ginger, and star anise in the cavity, and place it breast side up on a plate. (If cooking chicken parts, just add the other ingredients to the plate.) Bring the water in the steamer to a boil, add the chicken on its plate, cover, and steam until the juices show just a trace of pink, about 30 minutes for a whole fryer and 20 minutes for cut-up parts. Remove the chicken from the steamer and let it cool slightly before smoking, or refrigerate overnight. Reserve the (rather salty) juices for another purpose.

Line a wok and its lid with heavy-duty aluminum foil, letting the excess hang over the edges for now. Set a small wire rack (round or square, whatever will hold the chicken an inch or two off the bottom) in the wok. Combine the tea, rice, sugar, and cinnamon and scatter into the space under the rack. Lay the chicken breast side up on the rack, and turn the heat under the wok to medium. Turn on the kitchen fan if you have one, or open up the kitchen windows for ventilation. In a few minutes the sugar and rice will begin to smolder. At this point, cover the wok and crimp the edges of the 2 sheets of foil together. Leave a tiny gap for the smoke to vent so you can monitor the heat. Reduce the heat to medium-low and cook 15 minutes. Turn off the heat and let stand another 5 minutes, then uncrimp the foil and remove the lid. Remove the chicken and the rack and promptly wrap up the burnt stuff in the foil. Let the package cool before putting it in the trash.

Serve the chicken warm or cool, carved into pieces Western style or hacked into sections through the bone with a cleaver, Chinese style.

Stir-Fried Crab with Black Bean Sauce

■ *Serves 3 to 4 with other dishes*

One of the favorite Cantonese ways to prepare just about anything that comes out of the water is in black bean sauce. The black beans in this case are not ordinary dried black beans, but soybeans that have been partially fermented and preserved in a soft state with salt. When chopped and added to stir-fried dishes or sauces, they act like little nuggets of soy sauce. Look for them in half-pound plastic bags (usually labeled "salted black bean") or half-kilogram cylindrical cardboard packages (the excellent Yang Jiang brand) in Asian groceries; they will keep indefinitely at room temperature.

1 live Dungeness crab, 1¹⁄₂ to 2 pounds, or 2 pounds live blue crabs

1 tablespoon minced ginger

1 tablespoon minced green onion

1¹⁄₂ teaspoons minced garlic

1 tablespoon Chinese fermented black beans, finely chopped

2 tablespoons soy sauce

2 tablespoons Chinese rice wine or dry sherry

¹⁄₂ cup unsalted chicken stock or water

1 tablespoon oil

1 teaspoon cornstarch dissolved in 2 tablespoons water

Shredded green onion tops or cilantro leaves, for garnish

WHICH BEER?

Pilsner or hefeweizen.

Place the crab in a deep pot with cool water to cover by several inches. Cover the pot and set over high heat. Check after about 8 minutes; by the time the water reaches 100°F the crab will be dead but not cooked. Remove the crab with tongs (leave the water heating) and rinse it with cold water to stop the cooking. Grasp the underside and legs of the crab with one hand and pull off the top shell (carapace) with the other. Pull out and reserve the fat and organs from the corners of the top shell, rinse the shell well, and return it to the pot to cook until bright red, another 5 minutes or so.

To clean the crab, remove the triangular "apron" on the underside, being careful of the spines hidden underneath. Remove the jaws, the gills (the gray, feathery pieces on each side of the body) and all the spongy greenish tissue in the center of the body. Rinse the crab well until nothing but shell and meat remains. Split the body in half with the knife if you have not already done so, then cut between the legs to make 10 pieces, each containing part of the body.

Combine the ginger, onion, garlic, and black beans in a bowl. Combine the soy sauce, wine, and stock in another bowl, together with a tablespoon or two of the reserved crab fat if you like.

Heat a wok over low heat for a couple of minutes, then turn the heat to high. Add the oil in a thin stream around the edge of the wok. Add the ginger mixture and stir-fry a few seconds. Add the crab pieces and stir-fry until the shells begin to turn red. Add the soy sauce mixture. Cover and cook until the shells are entirely red and all the exposed meat is opaque white; lift the lid every minute or so and toss the mixture to ensure even cooking.

Stir in the cornstarch mixture and cook until the sauce thickens and becomes glossy. Transfer to a serving platter and take a moment to arrange the pieces in a more or less lifelike pattern. Set the boiled shell on top and garnish the platter with green onions or cilantro.

VARIATION The same sauce works well on lobster, as well as quicker-cooking items like shrimp, clams, squid, or cubes of chicken. For the latter, stir-fry the seafood first until nearly done, then remove it while you assemble and reduce the sauce. Return the seafood to the sauce just to reheat.

Hunan "Smoked" Pork with Leeks

■ *Serves 2 to 4*

One of my favorite dishes in Chinese restaurants serving Hunan and Sichuan cuisines is slices of pink, hamlike cured pork with stir-fried leeks in a chile and garlic sauce. Although this is usually listed in English as "smoked pork," I'm not at all sure that the meat they serve is actually smoked; my guidebook to deciphering Chinese menus translates the key characters on the menu as là ròu, "cured pork," and I don't always taste smoke in the restaurant versions. Having tried it both ways, with and without smoking, I definitely recommend the former, which is easy to accomplish on the stovetop with a wok and some aluminum foil. If you have some other form of hot smoker available, feel free to use it. Note that this recipe makes more smoked pork than you need for the stir-fry. I'm sure you can find other uses for it.

WHICH BEER?

Amber ale or Märzen.

1 pound boneless pork loin, or a similarly sized single muscle from the fresh leg

Kosher salt or curing salt, for brine (see Note)

Brown sugar, for brine

Sichuan peppercorns, for brine

3 tablespoons raw rice

2 tablespoons white or brown sugar

1 tablespoon tea leaves (optional)

2 medium leeks

1 to 2 tablespoons oil

1 tablespoon minced garlic

1 tablespoon minced ginger

$1/4$ teaspoon bottled chile paste or red pepper flakes

1 tablespoon soy sauce

$1/2$ cup unsalted chicken stock

Scant teaspoon vinegar

Scant teaspoon sugar

1 teaspoon cornstarch dissolved in 1 tablespoon water

Trim as much fat as possible from the meat. Choose a container that will hold the meat snugly and add water to cover, measuring the water as you go. Remove the meat and stir in 2 tablespoons salt, 1½ tablespoons brown sugar, and ½ teaspoon Sichuan peppercorns per cup of water. (If using a sealable plastic bag, a 2-cup batch of brine is about right.) Return the meat to the brine, seal the bag, and refrigerate overnight. If not smoking or otherwise cooking the meat that day, drain and rinse it, wrap it tightly, and refrigerate for up to 2 more days.

To smoke the pork, drain and rinse it, if you have not already done so; pat dry. Line a wok and its lid with heavy-duty aluminum foil, letting the excess hang over the edges for now. Set a small wire rack (round or square, whatever will hold the meat an inch or two off the bottom) in the wok. Sprinkle the rice, sugar, and tea into the space under the rack, lay the meat on the rack, and turn the heat under the wok to medium. Turn on the kitchen fan if you have one, or open up the kitchen windows for ventilation. In a few minutes the sugar and rice will begin to smolder. At this point, cover the wok and crimp the edges of the two sheets of foil together. Leave a tiny gap for the smoke to vent so you can monitor the heat. Reduce the heat to low and cook 30 minutes; most of the smoke will be gone after about half that time, but the meat should continue to roast in the enclosed space. Turn off the heat, let the wok cool a bit, then uncrimp the foil and remove the lid. The pork should register at least 140°F on an instant-read thermometer; reseal the foil and cook a little longer if it is still underdone. (The pork can be prepared 2 or 3 days ahead of time and refrigerated.) Wrap up the burnt stuff promptly in the foil and let the package cool before putting it in the trash.

Set a wok on the lowest possible heat to preheat. Trim the root ends of the leeks and remove any beat-up outer leaves; don't worry about washing them for now. Starting at the root end, slice the leeks diagonally about ½ inch thick up to the point where they start to turn from white to green. From here on, remove the tougher, darker green outside leaves and continue slicing the paler parts inside. Transfer the slices to a deep bowl of water, break up the outer rings to expose any dirt hidden between the layers, and let stand for a few minutes before lifting the leeks out of the water (leaving any dirt behind) and into a colander to drain.

Slice about 4 ounces of the pork ⅛ inch thick across the grain. Cut the slices into bite-size pieces. Turn the heat under the wok to medium-high and add a tablespoon or so of oil. Add the drained leeks and cook, without browning, until they begin to soften. Add the garlic, ginger, chile paste, liquids, and sugar and bring to a simmer. Add the meat slices and simmer until the leeks are tender. Taste the sauce and adjust the seasoning, then stir in the cornstarch mixture and cook until the sauce is glossy and slightly thickened. Serve immediately, with rice.

NOTE Commercial hams and many other cured pork products include a little sodium or potassium nitrite in the cure, to maintain the pink color in the cooked meat. Premixed curing salts with the proper proportion of nitrite are sold by commercial butcher supply houses, but you may also find them in small quantities in an Asian market, usually among the little plastic bags of spice mixes. I have used the Two Fishes brand from Hong Kong, which lists only one ingredient, "curing salt," but presumably contains nitrite, because my smoked pork comes out nice and pink like Canadian bacon.

If you can't find or don't want to use nitrites, just use kosher salt; the meat will taste the same, though it will look like ordinary cooked pork.

VARIATION To prepare the pork without the smoking step, cure the meat as above (if you want to add a bit of liquid smoke, I won't tell), and roast it to an internal temperature of 140°F. Let cool before slicing.

If you really don't want to bother with the curing and smoking step but get a hankering for this dish, try slices of smoked ham, parboiled in plain water if they are too salty.

Stir-Fried Vegetables and Tofu with Oyster Sauce

■ *Serves 2 to 4*

Usually labeled "home-style bean curd" or something similar on Chinese restaurant menus, this is one of my family's standard choices whether we are ordering takeout or cooking our own. Restaurant versions often use fried tofu, but we like it best with plain. Note that only the vegetables are actually stir-fried; the tofu cubes would break apart if tossed that vigorously, so they are added last to simmer in the sauce.

1 carton (14 ounces) tofu, regular or firm

2 tablespoons soy sauce

1 broccoli crown, about 5 ounces

1 tablespoon minced ginger

1 tablespoon minced garlic

2 green onions, white parts minced, tops sliced

1 cup unsalted chicken stock

1 tablespoon oyster sauce

1 to 2 tablespoons oil

1 medium carrot, peeled and sliced

1/2 medium yellow onion, cut into 1-inch squares

1 teaspoon cornstarch dissolved in 1 tablespoon water

WHICH BEER?
Just about any (let the rest of the menu guide you).

Set a wok over the lowest heat to warm. Drain the tofu. Cut the block in half lengthwise, then split each rectangle diagonally so it forms triangles when you slice it crosswise. Sprinkle the tofu pieces with 1 tablespoon of the soy sauce. Slice across the broccoli stem where it begins to branch, then continue slicing toward the top, letting the bite-size florets fall away. Include as much of the sliced stem as you like.

Combine the ginger, garlic, and minced green onion (not the tops) in a small bowl. Measure the stock in a 1-cup or larger measuring cup and add the oyster sauce and remaining 1 tablespoon soy sauce.

Turn the heat under the wok to high and add the oil. Add the minced ingredients and stir until fragrant, a few seconds. Add the carrots and onions and stir-fry briefly to coat with the oil. Stir the liquids (the oyster sauce tends to stick to the bottom of the cup), add to the wok, cover, and steam until the vegetables are crisp-tender, about 4 minutes.

Drain the tofu again and add it to the wok with the green onion tops. Stir gently to fold the tofu into the sauce, and cook until reheated. Push the contents to the edge of the wok; stir the cornstarch mixture and add it to the sauce in the center. Boil until the sauce is glossy and lightly thickened. Transfer to a serving platter or shallow bowl and serve immediately.

NOTE This dish gets a lot of its character from oyster sauce (which for some reason has to be labeled "oyster-flavored sauce"), a thick, brownish liquid based on oysters, usually with some cornstarch and caramel added. The widely available Lee Kum Kee brand from Hong Kong is certainly adequate, though some of the more expensive brands sold in Asian markets offer a more intense oyster flavor.

VARIATION Feel free to vary the vegetables. Substitute other green vegetables like "baby" or Shanghai bok choy or the small, white-stemmed choy sum for the broccoli. Other good additions include squares of red or green bell pepper, mushrooms (either fresh or the canned straw mushrooms from Asia), sliced bamboo shoots (ditto), and canned baby corn.

Oven-Steamed Fish with Black Mushrooms

■ *Serves 4*

Baking in small packages of parchment, what the French call en papillote, *is sometimes translated as "oven steaming," and it does combine some of the best qualities of steaming with the ease of baking. Enclosed in a nearly air-tight package, the fish and seasonings cook quickly, retaining all their natural moisture in a sauce contained in each package. Here, fish fillets cook with the classic Chinese seasonings for fish (ginger and green onions) plus the earthy flavor of dried black (shiitake) mushrooms. Try using lean fish like rockfish, snapper, thicker soles and flounders, farmed striped bass, or tilapia; moderately rich fish like mahi-mahi, trout, or catfish; or salmon. About the only fish that don't take well to this method are firm, meaty "steak fish" like tuna, swordfish, and shark.*

6 good-sized dried black mushrooms

½ cup unsalted chicken stock

2 tablespoons Chinese rice wine or good dry sherry

1 tablespoon soy sauce

¼ teaspoon sugar (omit if your sherry is on the sweet side)

4 fillet portions lean to moderately rich fish, 5 to 7 ounces each

1-inch chunk fresh ginger, peeled, sliced, and cut into shreds

2 green onions, cut into 2-inch lengths and shredded lengthwise

WHICH BEER?
Amber ale, porter, or dry stout.

Soak the mushrooms in warm water to cover for at least 20 minutes. Drain and cut off the stems; cut the caps in ⅛-inch slices. Combine in a small saucepan with the stock, wine, soy sauce, and sugar and simmer until the mushrooms are tender. Remove the mushrooms with a slotted spoon and boil the liquid down by two thirds. Let cool.

Preheat the oven to 450°F. For each serving, fold a 12- by 16-inch sheet of baking parchment in half the short way. Crease the edges of the fold but not the entire fold. Open the parchment and lay a portion of fish on one side of the fold, spoon or brush a quarter of the sauce over the fish, and top with a quarter of the ginger and green onion shreds, and a quarter of the mushrooms. Fold the other side of the paper over all. Starting at the edge of the fold nearest you, fold the corner in toward the center of the packet and crease; then fold the newly created corner toward the center and crease. Continue with a series of folds, forming a half oval and creasing each fold well to seal. Finish with a twist at the opposite corner.

Bake the packages on a baking sheet until puffy and browned, about 8 minutes. Transfer to individual plates to be opened at the table (either slit the paper open along the edge and slide the contents out onto the plate or open the top and eat the fish from the paper). Serve with rice and a simple vegetable.

Jasmine Rice

■ *Makes 4¹/₂ cups*

My favorite everyday white rice is Thai jasmine, a long-grain variety with a subtle, slightly nutty fragrance that is not anywhere near as flowery as the name would suggest. It's now almost as easy to find as domestic long-grain rice, although you may have to buy it in 10-pound or larger bags.

Experiment to find the amount of water that makes rice of the texture you like in the pot you use. The proportions here suit my pot, which is heavy aluminum and almost as deep as it is wide, and my family's taste for rice on the sticky side. Use up to ¹/₂ cup less water if you prefer your rice firmer and more separate.

I don't wash my rice. Go ahead and wash yours if you like.

2 cups jasmine rice

3¹/₂ cups water

Combine the rice and water in a heavy covered pan. Bring to a boil over medium heat; when water comes sputtering out around the lid, reduce the heat as low as it will go and cook 16 minutes. Lift the lid and check the rice; there should be no water showing around the edges, and you should see several small holes in the top surface. Loosen the rice with a wooden spoon or rice paddle, replace the cover, and let stand 5 minutes before serving.

Satay *(Skewered Grilled Meats)*

■ *Serves 6 to 8 as an appetizer, 3 to 4 as an entrée*

Satay (sometimes spelled saté) is not a single dish but a whole genre of cooking popular all across Southeast Asia. Wherever people gather, in the marketplace, on street corners, or in special areas devoted to stalls selling cooked food, someone is likely to have a charcoal grill going, cooking small pieces of meat on skewers and serving them with a spicy peanut sauce.

I like to serve satay as an appetizer when grilling something else as an entrée; the quick-cooking skewers give hungry guests something to nibble on while the main dish cooks. But a larger quantity of satay, plus rice and a vegetable dish or two, makes a fine meal. Indoors, your choices include cooking the skewers under the broiler, on a stovetop grill, or at the table if you have an appropriate tabletop grill.

WHICH BEER?

Your favorite lager.

Satay Marinade I or II (recipes follow)

1 pound boneless pork shoulder or loin, lamb, chicken breast or leg, or turkey

Peanut Sauce (recipe follows)

Prepare your choice of marinade. Slice the meat across the grain, ⅛ to ¼ inch thick. Toss the meat in the marinade and let it stand for at least an hour, preferably several hours. If using bamboo or wooden skewers, soak them in water while the meat marinates to prevent burning.

Remove the meat from the refrigerator at least half an hour before cooking. Thread the meat onto skewers in a wave pattern, then stretch it out so it makes as even a layer as possible. Grill over a hot fire until just done but still moist, about 5 minutes. Serve with Peanut Sauce.

Satay Marinade I (with Tamarind)

▓ *For 1 pound of meat*

2 teaspoons coriander seed or ground coriander

1 teaspoon dried galangal flakes, 2 or 3 slices dried galangal, or 1 teaspoon ground galangal

1 tablespoon chopped ginger

1 tablespoon chopped garlic

2 tablespoons fish sauce

2 tablespoons tamarind water (see Note)

If using whole coriander and galangal, grind them to a powder in a spice grinder. Mince the ginger and garlic together until very fine, or better still, pound them in a mortar to an almost liquid paste. (The quantity is too small to do this in a blender.) Combine the ginger-garlic paste with the ground spices , fish sauce, and tamarind water in a bowl large enough to hold the meat.

NOTE To make tamarind water, either dissolve a ½-inch cube of tamarind pulp (sold in blocks) in warm water and strain, or use 1 teaspoon Indian-style tamarind concentrate (no straining needed).

Satay Marinade II (with Coconut Milk)

▓ *For 1 pound of meat*

½ cup unsweetened coconut cream

½ teaspoon ground turmeric

2 or 3 inches lemongrass top, roughly chopped

2 teaspoons fish sauce

Combine the ingredients in a small saucepan and bring to a simmer. Remove from the heat and let cool before adding the meat.

NOTE "Coconut cream" means the cream skimmed from a can of coconut milk, not the stuff bartenders use to make piña coladas.

Peanut Sauce

■ *Makes 2 cups*

The dried shrimp is optional but gives a nice flavor to this sauce, much better than the smell of the raw ingredient. If you omit it, add a splash of fish sauce.

$1/4$ cup peanut or other vegetable oil

$1/4$ cup chopped garlic

$1/3$ cup chopped ginger

$1/4$ cup dried shrimp, coarsely chopped (optional)

$1/4$ cup sweetened shredded coconut

$1/4$ cup tamarind water (see Note, page 137) or citrus juice

$1/4$ teaspoon cayenne, or $1/2$ teaspoon bottled chile-garlic paste

1 cup peanut butter

$1/4$ cup chopped cilantro

Heat the oil in a skillet (nonstick is handy) over moderate heat. Add the garlic, ginger, and dried shrimp and fry gently, adjusting the heat so the garlic and ginger sizzle but do not brown too quickly. When the garlic begins to color, after 8 to 10 minutes, add the coconut and cook for another 2 minutes. Add the tamarind water and cayenne, and stir in the peanut butter. Cook, stirring frequently to prevent scorching, for another 5 minutes. Remove the pan from the heat and let the sauce cool enough to taste it. It should be pleasantly hot but balanced by the sweetness of the coconut and the tart flavor of the tamarind. Adjust the seasonings accordingly, adding a little sugar if necessary. Stir in the cilantro and serve warm or at room temperature as a dipping sauce for pork or chicken satay or other grilled meats or poultry.

Green Papaya Salad

■ *Serves 4*

One of the most common "vegetables" in much of Southeast Asia is actually a fruit, the papaya. With a flavor and texture somewhere between cucumber and raw cabbage, a full-size but unripe papaya is ideal for cutting into fine ribbons or shreds as the base for a salad. The papaya variety most commonly used for salad is considerably bigger and less pear-shaped than the sweet variety; it looks more like a small watermelon with a uniformly green skin. An unripe sweet papaya is a distant second choice. If a whole papaya is too much to buy and the store does not sell cut pieces, look for packages of shredded green papaya in the freezer section.

Top this salad with your choice of meats—cold cooked chicken or pork, shrimp, or a combination.

1 tablespoon oil

1 clove garlic, sliced and cut into slivers

1 cup shredded green papaya

1 medium carrot, shredded

1 green onion, cut into 1-inch pieces and shredded lengthwise

1/2 cup shredded cooked chicken, cold sliced pork, or cooked shrimp

About 1/3 cup Chile-Lime Dressing (recipe follows)

Mint leaves and chopped toasted peanuts, for garnish

WHICH BEER?

Lager or not-too-bitter ale, depending on the rest of the menu.

In a small pan, combine the oil and garlic and cook over low heat until the garlic just begins to brown. Remove from the heat. Combine the papaya, carrot, green onion, and meat with about 1/3 cup of the dressing. Add the garlic and oil and mix well. Let stand for about 15 minutes for the best flavor. To serve, arrange on a plate with some of the meat on top, and garnish with mint and peanuts.

Chile-Lime Dressing

■ *Makes about 1 cup*

Use leftovers as a dipping sauce or dressing for cold noodles.

2 cloves garlic

1 or 2 small fresh chiles, preferably red, stem, seeds, and ribs removed

2 tablespoons best-quality fish sauce

2 tablespoons lime juice

3 tablespoons sugar, or to taste

$1/2$ cup hot water

Chop the garlic and chile together finely. Combine in a bowl with the remaining ingredients, stir to dissolve the sugar, and adjust the flavors to taste.

TECHNIQUE NOTE The fine julienne cutter of a mandoline (see page 88) is ideal for shredding the papaya and carrot. Otherwise, either cut them by hand into the finest shreds you can manage, or grate on a box grater, trying to get the longest, thinnest pieces you can.

Stuffed Squid Curry

■ *Serves 2 to 4, with other dishes*

Like many Southeast Asian curries, this one has a lot of spicy broth and is meant to go with a lot of rice. Even so, you are likely to have some broth left over after eating all the squid, but it will keep for several days in the refrigerator.

You can chop the stuffing ingredients in a food processor or blender, but it works just as well to chop everything together on a cutting board. Start with the hardest items (lemongrass, ginger, garlic), then gradually add the rest and keep chopping. Even if you're not especially fast with a knife, you will probably save time compared to setting up and cleaning the machine.

1 cup canned coconut milk

1 pound squid, fresh if possible

1 stalk lemongrass

1 clove garlic, minced

1 tablespoon minced ginger

2 green onions, white parts minced, tops sliced

1 tablespoon Thai red curry paste

1 or 2 slices fresh or dried galangal (optional)

2 tablespoons fish sauce

$^1/_2$ cup tender sprigs of basil, preferably the purple-stemmed Thai variety

WHICH BEER?
Something with a bit of sweetness to balance the heat—amber ale, Märzen, dunkel.

Pour the coconut milk into a measuring pitcher and let it stand while you prepare the squid and stuffing.

Clean the squid, peeling off the thin spotted skin. Try to keep the fins attached to the bodies when you remove the skins. Chop the tentacles as finely as possible and set aside.

Cut a teaspoon of very thin slices off the bottom of the lemongrass; cut the rest into 2-inch pieces. Mince the slices as finely as possible with the garlic and ginger. Add the minced (white) green onion and squid tentacles and chop the whole mixture to a loose paste. Using a spoon or a pastry bag, stuff the squid bodies half full with the mixture, and close the ends with toothpicks. Refrigerate if not cooking right away.

Spoon 2 tablespoons of "cream" from the coconut milk into a deep skillet or wok. Add the curry paste, galangal (if used), and the rest of the lemongrass, bruised with the side of a large knife. Cook over low heat, stirring frequently, until the mixture is nearly dry. Meanwhile, discard as much of the remaining coconut cream as you like (or save it for Satay Marinade II, page 137); add water to the remaining milk to make 1½ cups total liquid. Add the thinned coconut milk and the fish sauce to the pan and bring to a simmer. Add the stuffed squid and simmer until it goes through the tough stage and back to tender, about 25 minutes (cut one open and taste it, checking for doneness of the stuffing at the same time). Stir in the basil and sliced green onions, taste the sauce for seasoning and correct if necessary, and strain the sauce into a deep bowl. Remove the toothpicks from the squid before adding them to the bowl. The lemongrass and galangal can go into the bowl or not, as you like, but in any case are not meant to be eaten.

VARIATION Squid stuffed with pork is very common in Southeast Asia. Substitute 2 ounces ground pork for the squid tentacles in the previous recipe. You can fix the tentacles back onto the stuffed squid, or simply add them to the curry to cook alongside the stuffed bodies, or you can use them for another dish entirely.

Street-Style Grilled Chicken

■ *Serves 4*

One of the favorite street foods all across Southeast Asia is grilled chicken, usually marinated in some form of spiced soy sauce. In Vietnam, the marinade may include cinnamon or five-spice powder; in Malaysia and Singapore, rice wine and oyster sauce; in Indonesia, tamarind; and so on. And of course, no two cooks make it exactly the same. This version is basically Thai, especially the sweetish red chile sauce that accompanies the chicken. If you don't feel like making your own, you can buy bottled "sweet chili sauce for chicken" in most Asian groceries. If you find the bottled version too sweet, as I often do, you can cut it with a little vinegar. Similarly, if my sauce is not sweet enough for your taste, feel free to add more sugar.

A mortar and pestle works best for extracting all the flavor from the spices and aromatics, but you can also use ground spices or a spice grinder and mince the other ingredients by hand.

MARINADE

1 teaspoon coriander seed, ground

1/2 teaspoon white peppercorns, ground

2 teaspoons minced lemongrass

3 good-sized slices ginger

2 cloves garlic

1/4 cup soy sauce

1/2 teaspoon sugar

■

1 small frying chicken, or 2 to 3 pounds chicken parts

SWEET CHILE SAUCE

1/2 cup rice or cider vinegar

1/4 cup sugar

1 tablespoon red pepper flakes

WHICH BEER?
A dry-finishing lager or pale ale,
if not too hoppy.

1 large clove garlic, minced

¼ teaspoon kosher salt, or to taste

If using a mortar and pestle, grind the marinade spices first, then add the lemongrass, ginger, and garlic and pound to a paste. Transfer to a bowl large enough to hold the chicken and stir in the soy sauce and sugar. Otherwise, mince the lemongrass, ginger, and garlic together, transfer to the marinating bowl, and add the spices, soy sauce, and sugar.

Rinse the chicken and pat dry. Divide it into whatever form you find most convenient for grilling (split down the back and flattened, split into halves, "semi-boned" like the quail on page 154, or cut up into small parts), trimming off excess skin and fat. Toss the chicken in the marinade to coat evenly. Marinate 30 minutes to overnight; refrigerate if holding for more than an hour before grilling.

Combine the chile sauce ingredients in a small saucepan and bring to a boil. (Watch out—the chile fumes can be powerful.) Reduce the heat and simmer until the sauce is syrupy. Remove from the heat, set aside until cool enough to taste, and adjust with more sugar or salt if desired.

Prepare a medium-hot fire in a covered charcoal or gas grill. Remove the chicken from the refrigerator 20 to 30 minutes before cooking. Grill, basting occasionally with the marinade remaining in the bowl, until the chicken juices run clear and the breast and thigh meat register at least 155°F, about 15 minutes per side. Let rest for a few minutes before carving. Serve with individual bowls of the sweet chile sauce.

Bulgogi
(Korean Grilled Beef with Garnishes)

■ *Serves 4 to 6*

Variously spelled bulgogi, bulkogi, *or other variations, this dish of thinly sliced beef in a sesame and soy marinade is Korea's best known specialty and is probably on the menu of every Korean restaurant in North America (except those catering to vegetarians). In some restaurants, diners cook the meat themselves on a hibachi-like grill at the table, which you can do at home if you have an appropriate tabletop grill or even an electric skillet.*

Short ribs, especially the thin crosscut version called flanken ribs, are the traditional cut for this dish, and while they have lots of flavor, I find them hard to eat with chopsticks. I prefer a more tender boneless cut such as the small, tender flatiron muscle in the chuck or various parts of the sirloin. If you're not sure, ask for something suitable for stir-frying.

By itself, bulgogi would just be another version of soy-flavored grilled beef. What makes it special is the assortment of little dishes set out to accompany the beef and rice. I have seen as many as seventeen items served along with bulgogi in restaurants. Kimchi, the fiery pickle that seems to be equal parts cabbage and chile powder, is a given; it's widely available wherever Asian foods are sold, so I suggest buying it already made. Bean-sprout salads are another constant, often several varieties, as are spinach and cucumber salads. I have suggested a modest assortment, including one for the adventurous made from tiny dried fish.

In traditional family style, everyone helps themselves to meat and garnishes with chopsticks; if you prefer, you can provide serving spoons.

1 tablespoon sesame seeds

2 cloves garlic, crushed or minced

1 tablespoon minced ginger

1 green onion, coarsely chopped

1$\frac{1}{2}$ tablespoons sugar

$\frac{1}{4}$ cup soy sauce

WHICH BEER?
Go for the malt flavors here—
amber ale, dunkel,
maybe a sweet stout.

1 tablespoon Asian sesame oil

1 pound tender beef (flatiron or sirloin)

GARNISHES

Kimchi (available at Asian groceries)

Marinated Bean Sprouts (recipe follows)

Sesame Spinach (recipe follows)

Cucumber Salad (recipe follows)

Chile-Fried Little Fish (recipe follows)

3 or 4 green onions, cut into 2-inch lengths (optional)

■

Cooked rice

Toast the sesame seeds in a dry skillet, stirring or shaking frequently, until lightly browned and fragrant. Transfer to a medium bowl and combine with the garlic, ginger, green onion, sugar, soy sauce, and sesame oil.

Slice the beef thinly across the grain. To tell if it is tender enough to cook as is, dip a piece in the marinade and quickly sauté it in a hot skillet (the one you used for the sesame seeds) and cook to medium-rare, 30 seconds to a minute per side. If this results in a chewy cut, tenderize a slice by scoring it with shallow X-shaped cuts, whacking it with the side of a cleaver or a meat pounder, or both. Slice and, if necessary, tenderize the remaining meat and add the slices to the marinade. Marinate overnight in the bowl or in a sealable plastic bag.

At your leisure, prepare the garnishes.

Set the table with a rice bowl or small plate for each diner and place the garnishes in the middle, within everyone's reach. Preheat a stovetop or tabletop grill and have a warm platter ready to receive the meat. Grill the meat slices to medium-rare or to your liking, 30 seconds to a minute per side. Serve immediately with rice.

Marinated Bean Sprouts

1/2 pound (2 cups) mung bean or soybean sprouts

1$\frac{1}{2}$ teaspoons Asian sesame oil

Pinch of kosher salt and freshly ground black pepper

1 or 2 green onions, thinly sliced diagonally

Parboil the bean sprouts in lightly salted water for 2 minutes; drain thoroughly. Combine the sesame oil, salt, and pepper in a medium mixing bowl. Add the drained sprouts and green onions and toss to blend.

Sesame Spinach

1 bunch fresh spinach (8 to 10 ounces)

2 teaspoons Asian sesame oil

1 teaspoon soy sauce

$\frac{1}{8}$ teaspoon fine red pepper flakes, or to taste

1 teaspoon toasted sesame seeds

Separate the larger outer leaves from the spinach and trim their stems; leave the smaller leaves attached to the roots and trim any withered stems. Wash the spinach well in several changes of water. Parboil in lightly salted water until wilted, about 30 seconds; retrieve and rinse with cold water, then squeeze gently and leave to drain thoroughly in a colander.

Combine the sesame oil, soy sauce, and red pepper flakes in a mixing bowl; add the spinach and toss to coat evenly with the dressing. Transfer to a serving dish and garnish with the sesame seeds.

Cucumber Salad

■

1 pickling cucumber, about 4 inches long

1 clove garlic

Heaping $\frac{1}{2}$ teaspoon kosher salt

$1\frac{1}{2}$ teaspoons rice vinegar

$\frac{1}{4}$ teaspoon sugar

Slice the cucumber very thinly ($\frac{1}{8}$ to $\frac{1}{16}$ inch). Slice the garlic to about the same thickness. Combine in a bowl, sprinkle with the salt, and toss to distribute the salt evenly. Let stand 30 minutes to several hours, then rinse with cold water and drain well on a cloth or paper towel. Combine in a bowl with the vinegar and sugar and let stand until ready to serve.

Chile-Fried Little Fish

■

1 cup oil

$\frac{1}{3}$ cup tiny dried fish (may be labeled anchovy, whitebait, or simply dried fish)

$\frac{1}{2}$ teaspoon fine red pepper flakes (called "sausage grind" in some spice shops; or sift regular flakes through a coarse sieve)

Heat the oil in a wok or small saucepan over medium heat until a fish sizzles on contact. Add the fish and cook, stirring occasionally, until golden brown and quite crisp, 2 to 3 minutes. Drain briefly on absorbent paper, then dust with red pepper. Serve warm or at room temperature.

NOTE When the oil cools, you can strain it through a fine sieve, store it in a jar, and use it for frying or stir-frying other seafood.

East-West Crab Gyoza

▨ *Makes about 18 (4 to 6 appetizer servings)*

While most older Asian-Americans turn up their noses at cheese (and dairy products in general), their kids have grown up with it, and a few cheese-based dishes like this one have become standard items in restaurants where East meets West. A little cream cheese give a luscious texture to the crab filling for the traditional browned and steamed dumplings known as potstickers in Chinese restaurants and gyoza in Japanese. For a dipping sauce, you could use the traditional potsticker condiments of soy sauce, vinegar, and chile oil, but I like to use a Vietnamese-style nuoc cham.

FILLING

3 ounces crabmeat (about $\frac{1}{2}$ cup)

$1\frac{1}{2}$ ounces cream cheese

1 teaspoon minced ginger

1 tablespoons minced green onion

Freshly ground white pepper

Pinch of kosher salt

▨

1 package round potsticker wraps (may be labeled gyoza or sue gow wraps)

2 to 3 tablespoons oil

Nuoc Cham (recipe follows), or simply set out soy sauce, chile oil, and seasoned rice vinegar for do-it-yourself dipping sauces

WHICH BEER?

Pilsner or hefeweizen.

Combine the filling ingredients and season to taste. For each dumpling, place a generous teaspoon of filling off center on a wrapper. Moisten the edge of the wrapper lightly and fold it in half over the filling, pinching the layers together opposite the fold. Grab a bit of the near side of the wrapper and pleat it toward the center, then pinch the pleat together with the far (flat) side. Repeat with 2 or 3 pleats toward the center and an equal number on the opposite side. The dumpling will curve away from the pleated side in the process, which is intentional.

Set the finished dumplings on a dry plate or sheet pan, pleats up, and keep them covered with a towel to prevent drying out while you make the rest.

Choose a nonstick skillet with a very flat bottom and a tight-fitting lid. Have ready ⅓ cup of water for a 10-inch skillet, ½ cup for a 12-inch. Coat the pan with a light layer of oil and heat over medium-high heat until the oil gets noticeably thinner. Add the dumplings flat side down, at least ⅛ inch apart. Cook until the bottoms are golden brown, then add the water (watch out for splattering) and immediately cover the pan. Cook until the water is nearly gone and the dumpling skins are tender, 6 to 8 minutes. Uncover and continue cooking until the liquid is gone and the bottoms become crisp in the remaining oil. Remove with a spatula, arrange on a serving platter or individual plates, and serve immediately, with dipping sauce.

NOTE This makes more gyoza than you can cook in one pan; figure about a dozen at a time in a 10-inch skillet, 16 to 18 in a 12-inch one.

Nuoc Cham *(Vietnamese Dipping Sauce)*

■ *Makes about 1 cup*

2 cloves garlic

1 small red or green chile

6 tablespoons best-quality fish sauce

2 tablespoons lime or lemon juice

2 tablespoons sugar

¼ cup hot water

½ teaspoon red chile paste or Sriracha paste

Finely mince the garlic and chile, or pound together in a mortar. Combine with the remaining ingredients. Adjust the flavors to taste.

Crab Roasted in the Shell

■ *Serves 2 to 4*

Roast crab, a whole, crisp-shelled Dungeness crab seasoned with pepper and drizzled with seasoned butter, has been a specialty of the An family's San Francisco restaurants Crustacean and Thanh Long since the early 1970s. Nearly everyone who orders the crab also orders a plate or two of garlic noodles. The recipes for both are closely guarded family secrets—each restaurant has a "secret" kitchen where this and other specialty dishes are prepared—and I don't claim to be in on the secret. But this version comes pretty close. I learned about the roasting technique from another San Francisco restaurateur, chef Andrea Froncillo of the Crab House on Pier 39.

Serving the butter sauce over the crab is more authentic, but I find it a little less messy to serve it in ramekins, steamed lobster style. Either way, this is messy finger food, so provide plenty of napkins and bowls for the crab shells. If you want to be really fancy, pass warm, damp washcloths at the end (you can warm them in a steamer on top of the stove while you are eating).

2 live or cooked Dungeness crabs, 1$\frac{1}{2}$ to 2 pounds each

2 tablespoons plus 1 teaspoon kosher salt

1 teaspoon freshly ground pepper (black, white, or a combination)

$\frac{1}{2}$ teaspoon ground Sichuan peppercorns

$\frac{1}{4}$ teaspoon garlic powder

2 tablespoons butter

WHICH BEER?
Pale ale, Pilsner.

If using live crabs, fill a good-sized pot with enough water to cover the crabs by a couple of inches. Add 2 tablespoons salt. Put in the crabs, cover, and bring the water almost to a boil over high heat. When the water is just about to boil, turn off the heat, let steep 15 minutes, and then remove the crabs and rinse them with cold water to stop the cooking (or surround them with ice cubes to chill even faster).

Clean the crabs as directed on page 126–27, leaving the body whole and the legs intact. Remove any loose organs from the top shells, but leave the fat pockets in the corners intact.

Preheat the oven to 325°F. Combine the remaining 1 teaspoon salt, pepper, Sichuan pepper, and garlic powder and sprinkle the mixture well over the crabs, reserving a pinch for the butter. Place right side up in a shallow roasting pan or rimmed sheet pan. Drain any water from the top shells and put them in the pan upside down. Bake until the shells are slightly browned and brittle, about 15 minutes. Meanwhile, melt the butter on top of the stove with the reserved crab seasonings.

Quarter the roasted crabs and arrange on a platter. Stir up to a tablespoon of the fat from the crab shells into the butter (taste it first; sometimes it can be bitter, in which case skip it), then either drizzle the butter over the crab pieces or pass it separately in ramekins. Add the top shells to the platter for decoration. Serve with Garlic Noodles (recipe follows), with individual shellfish crackers or nutcrackers.

Garlic Noodles

■ *Serves 2*

This is not much more than boiled noodles dressed with garlic-flavored oil, but it is addictively good. The recipe makes more garlic oil than you'll need, but it will keep for a couple of weeks, and you will probably find yourself using it long before that. If you are making the oil fresh for this dish, cook it in the same pan you will use for the noodles.

1 head garlic

1 cup peanut or corn oil

8 ounces thick, Chinese-style fresh egg noodles (regular mein)

¼ teaspoon kosher salt

Freshly ground black pepper, to taste

Pinch of ground Sichuan peppercorns

Separate and peel the garlic cloves. Slice as evenly as possible (a mandoline or other slicing device makes for the most consistent slices). Combine the garlic with the oil in a wok, deep skillet, or small saucepan and set over low heat. Cook as slowly as possible, stirring occasionally, until the garlic is golden brown. Strain through a heatproof sieve into a heatproof container; spread the garlic chips on a paper towel–lined plate to dry. Let the oil cool, then store it in a tightly sealed jar. If you like, chop a heaping teaspoon of the garlic chips as finely as possible, or grind them to fine crumbs in a mortar.

Boil the noodles in lightly salted water until tender; drain. Warm a generous tablespoon of the garlic oil in the wok and add the noodles, salt, black pepper, Sichuan pepper, and the optional chopped garlic bits. Toss to coat with the oil and serve immediately.

Watercress Salad with Soy-Glazed Quail

■ *Serves 6*

This dish illustrates two of the things I like best about Vietnamese cuisine: the deep, soul-satisfying flavor combination of caramelized sugar and pungent fish sauce, and the use of watercress, which I think Vietnamese cooks use to even better advantage than the French. Here, the sharp bitter-peppery taste of a simply dressed watercress salad is the perfect balance to the sweet, salty, gingery marinade on the quail.

CARAMEL SYRUP

$^1/_4$ cup sugar

$^1/_3$ cup water

2 tablespoons fish sauce

MARINADE

1 teaspoon minced garlic

1 teaspoon minced ginger

2 tablespoons Caramel Syrup, above

2 tablespoons fish sauce

2 tablespoons soy sauce

$^1/_2$ teaspoon sugar

$^1/_4$ teaspoon freshly ground black pepper

$^1/_4$ teaspoon five-spice powder

■

6 quail, fresh or thawed

1 tablespoon lemon juice

Kosher salt and freshly ground black pepper

1 tablespoon mild olive or peanut oil, or to taste

1 large bunch watercress, largest stems trimmed

WHICH BEER?

The watercress gives a good dose of bitterness here, so a not-too-hoppy amber or brown ale is in order.

At least 2 hours ahead of time, prepare the caramel syrup: Put the sugar in a dry, heavy-bottomed saucepan (2 quarts or larger). Place over medium heat and turn the exhaust fan to its maximum setting. When the sugar begins to melt around the edges, swirl (do not stir) the pan so the sugar melts evenly. Cook until the caramel darkens to a deep mahogany shade, then remove from the heat. Carefully pour in the water and fish sauce. The caramel will very likely seize into a solid mass; don't worry. Return the pan to the heat and bring the mixture back to a boil, swirling the pan, until the caramel is completely dissolved and the syrup is the color of strong coffee. Let cool, then transfer to a small jar and cover tightly. Store at room temperature.

Combine the marinade ingredients in a medium bowl. Split the quail, removing the backbones, breastbones, and ribs (see Technique Note). Add to the marinade bowl, turn to coat evenly, and marinate 30 minutes to several hours.

Preheat the oven to 375°F. Arrange the quail skin side up in a single layer in a shallow baking pan (or a large skillet with an ovenproof handle). Pour the marinade over the quail and roast 25 minutes.

While the quail roast, combine the lemon juice, salt, and pepper in a bowl and whisk to dissolve the salt, then whisk in the olive oil. Taste on a sprig of watercress and adjust the flavors to taste. Toss the watercress in this dressing and arrange on a platter, stems inward.

Remove the quail from the pan and set aside. Bring the pan juices to a boil on top of the stove and reduce to a syrupy glaze. Remove from the heat, return the quail to the pan, and turn to coat them with the glaze. Serve on the bed of watercress.

TECHNIQUE NOTE Partially boning the quail is no more difficult than boning other poultry. All the same muscles and bones are there; they are just a lot smaller. The following procedure takes longer to describe than to perform. Still, if you have never done this with any kind of bird, you might want to practice on a chicken first.

Poultry shears make quick work of splitting the birds and removing the backbones; lacking these, put each bird on its back, insert a chef's knife in the cavity, and cut down against the board first on one side of the backbone and then on the other. Now spread the bird out and lean on it with the heel of your hand to crack the ribs from the breastbone. Turn it skin side down, locate the rib cage and pelvic bones, and slide a boning knife or thin paring knife under the bones to separate them from the meat. When you get to the hip and shoulder joints, pop the thigh and wing bones out of the joints, and all the central bones should come away easily. Repeat on the other side, then cut as close as you can to one side of the breastbone to cut the bird in half. Cut away the breastbone and you are left with two half birds held together mainly by the skin, with only the leg and wing bones remaining.

FROM THE HOME OF THE CHILE PEPPER:

Beer and the Foods of Latin America and the American Southwest

The most dramatic global exchange of foods in history took place five centuries ago, after Columbus reached the Americas. Central and South America gave Europe the chile pepper in all its variations (*Capsicum* spp.), plus tomatoes, corn, squash, potatoes, turkey, and chocolate. Among the foods the New World got in return were domestic pigs and cattle and citrus fruits. It's hard to say who got the better end of the deal, but it moved Mexican cooking into the top rank with Chinese and French cuisine for making the best use of pork. A dish like *puerco en chile verde* made on either side of the Rio Grande is one of the greatest arguments for cross-cultural food exchanges.

Beer as we know it today was not part of the Columbian exchange, but during the global expansion of European-style brewing in the nineteenth century, beer found a welcome home in many Latin American countries. And Latin cuisines remain a favorite exploration ground for beer lovers today. Beyond the obvious chile heat, the mix of salty, tart, and sometimes sweet flavors calls for a moderate amount of sweetness and bitterness in the beer for balance (with the usual caveat about very bitter beers). In particular, I find myself reaching for a rich, malty lager in the Viennese and Bavarian styles with many of the dishes in this chapter. It's not just a matter of putting out the fire but of adding layers of flavor to match the complexity of the food.

Pantry Notes: Latin America and the American Southwest

CHILES, FRESH AND DRIED: All of the recipes in this book that call for chiles can be made with common varieties, including the small fresh serrano and jalapeño and the larger Anaheim/New Mexico/"long green" type. I prefer the flavor of serranos when I have the time (they are smaller and have thinner walls, making them harder to seed) but will settle for jalapeños when I am in a hurry. Most Mexican markets and some specialty produce markets also carry the dark green, cone-shaped chile poblano, the classic variety for roasting and stuffing or tearing into strips, and the small, lantern-shaped chile habanero, the hottest chile on the planet.

The basic small dried chile sold in supermarket spice jars is the dried serrano; it is much cheaper and is also likely to be fresher if bought in bulk at an Indian, Asian, or Latin grocery. Larger dried chiles used in the recipes in this chapter include the California or New Mexico red chile (sometimes called chile colorado or chile de la tierra,) 5 to 6 inches long and smooth; the slightly smaller, similarly shaped, but hotter chile gua-jillo; and the reddish-brown, wrinkled chile ancho, the ripened and dried form of the green pasilla. Ancho chiles are often labeled "pasilla" on the West Coast, although in Mexico that name belongs to a different chile.

DRIED CHILE PASTE: Most recipes using dried chiles call for toasting the chiles, soaking them in water for a long time, and finally grinding them with other ingredients, and they still come out with big flakes of red skin in the dish. Mike Marshall, virtuoso fiddler, mandolinist, and guitarist and a fine cook to boot, has figured out a better way: After soak-ing, he simply scrapes the flavorful pulp out of the chiles with a spoon, leaving the tough, waxy skins behind. It takes a little patience and a light touch, but it's still easier and less messy than setting up the blender, and it gives you more control over the moisture content. Brilliant!

TOMATILLOS: Although the name literally means "little tomatoes," these tart green fruits are a kind of ground cherry, used a lot like toma-toes in Mexican sauces. Once available only in cans, they are now widely available fresh wherever fresh chiles are sold. Look for tomatillos that are deep green, even turning a bit toward purple under their papery outer husks. They keep somewhat longer than fresh tomatoes, so grab some when you see them and plan to use them within a week or so.

Remove the husks and rinse off any sticky coating before roasting or simmering them, as the recipe directs.

QUESO AÑEJO (AGED CHEESE): One of the two basic types of cheese used in Mexican and other Latin American cooking, the other being a smoother melting type. Mexico's best-known *queso añejo* comes from the city of Cotija in Michoacán and is widely sold in Mexican markets here. It's a salty, crumbly white cheese, falling in texture and flavor somewhere between feta and Italian ricotta salata, and is typically crumbled over beans and other dishes. If you can't find it, try rinsed feta or ricotta salata.

For cheese to melt in quesadillas and similar dishes, I haven't tasted any Mexican imports or domestic Mexican-style cheeses that I like any better than Monterey Jack or domestic Muenster, so I use the latter.

Stuffed Jalapeño Chiles

■ *Makes 2 dozen*

Jalapeño "poppers" are now available frozen in every club store and most supermarkets, so why bother to make your own? Because the prefab versions are usually heavily battered and fried and filled with boring cheese. This lower-calorie baked version is still plenty rich, with two kinds of cheese. If you want additional crunch, you can dip them in egg and bread crumbs, but don't expect this coating to adhere completely to the smooth skin of the chiles.

Removing the ribs and seeds leaves a shell with only a fraction of the heat of the whole chile, but even so, some chiles remain searingly hot while others in the same batch can be pretty mild. That's part of the game with this dish— you never know when you're going to get a really hot one.

WHICH BEER?

Märzen or dunkel.

24 good-sized jalapeño chiles

2 ounces grated Jack or Muenster cheese

2 ounces grated feta or Mexican-style queso añejo de Cotija

1 tablespoon dried bread crumbs

1 beaten egg (optional)

½ cup dried bread crumbs (optional)

Slice the stem ends off the chiles. Roll each chile gently against the cutting board to loosen the seeds, then insert a vegetable peeler and carefully ream out as much as possible of the ribs and any remaining seeds.

Combine the cheeses and bread crumbs in a medium bowl. Holding the chiles over the bowl, gently stuff them with the cheese mixture, letting the excess fall back into the bowl. Refrigerate if not ready to cook.

Preheat the oven to 400°F. Lightly oil a baking sheet, or coat with cooking spray. Optional: For a crisp crust, dip the stuffed chiles in beaten egg, then roll them in bread crumbs.

Lay the stuffed chiles on the pan and bake until heated through and the coating is golden brown, about 15 minutes. Let cool slightly before serving.

Dried Shrimp Balls

■ *Makes 18*

Dried shrimp is one of those love-it-or-hate-it foods, but I am firmly in the former camp. As with sun-dried tomatoes and raisins, drying shrimp trans-forms them into a totally different ingredient from the fresh form. Here, they give their concentrated flavor to little fritter-like snacks that are mostly shrimp. The only published recipe I have seen for a similar dish is in Diana Kennedy's first book, Cuisines of Mexico, *and that has whole dried shrimp in a lot more batter. This is my attempt to re-create a version using ground shrimp that I was served some years ago in a private home in San Diego. The sauce is not especially Mexican, but I like the way it wraps around the flavor and texture of the shrimp balls without adding too much fat.*

Good dried shrimp are easier to find in Asian markets than Mexican. Although they are dried, they don't keep indefinitely. Look for the ones that are relatively plump and orange rather than shriveled and tan, and store any leftovers tightly sealed in a jar in the refrigerator.

$1/2$ cup ($1^1/2$ ounces) dried shrimp

1 tablespoon sesame tahini

2 tablespoons orange juice

Pinch of kosher salt

Tabasco, Sriracha, or other liquid chile
   sauce to taste

2 tablespoons flour

$1/2$ teaspoon baking powder

$1/4$ teaspoon kosher salt

1 or 2 serrano chiles, seeded and minced

1 egg

Oil, for pan-frying

WHICH BEER?
Pale lager or hefeweizen if serving
several beers; otherwise follow
the rest of the menu.

In a small bowl, soak the shrimp in hot water to cover for 15 minutes. Meanwhile, in another bowl, blend the tahini, orange juice, salt, and chile sauce to taste; thin with a few drops of water to a dipping consistency.

Combine the flour, baking powder, and salt in a medium bowl. Drain the shrimp and pound it to fine shreds in a mortar. This is easier to do in several batches; scoop out each batch into the bowl with the dry ingredients before grinding the next. Add the minced chiles and egg and stir just until well combined.

Fill a wok or small skillet with oil to a depth of about 1 inch. Heat until a pinch of the batter sizzles instantly on contact, then reduce the heat to low. Scoop up a teaspoon of the batter, smooth it into an oval with another teaspoon, and slide it into the hot oil. Continue forming and frying the balls without crowding, regulating the heat so they cook to golden brown in about a minute per side. Retrieve with a wire skimmer and drain on paper towels. Serve warm, with the tahini sauce for dipping.

Mushroom and Green Chile Quesadillas

■ *Serves 2 to 4*

While I prefer corn tortillas for most purposes, I always keep some flour tortillas on hand for a quick snack or lunch of quesadillas. Nothing could be simpler—heat up a skillet, throw in a tortilla, grate or slice some cheese, add a spoonful of salsa, fold, and toast. But sometimes I want to go to a little more trouble and make a more substantial quesadilla.

1 tablespoon olive oil

¼ pound mushrooms, sliced ¼ inch thick

1 green onion, sliced

Pinch of kosher salt

4 smallish (7- or 8-inch) flour tortillas

4 ounces sliced Jack, Muenster, or mild cheddar cheese

2 poblano or long green chiles, roasted, peeled, seeded, and cut into strips

About 12 epazote leaves (optional; see Note)

WHICH BEER?

Whatever is handy.

Heat the oil in a large skillet over medium-high heat. Add the mushrooms and sauté until they begin to give off a lot of liquid. Add the green onion, reduce the heat, and cook until the liquid disappears. Season the mushrooms with a pinch of salt and remove from the skillet. Wipe the skillet dry and lay in a tortilla. Add a quarter of the cheese on one side and top with mushrooms, chile strips, and a few epazote leaves. Fold the tortilla in half and toast until golden brown on both sides. Add more tortillas to the pan as space becomes available. Serve hot, whole or cut into wedges. Taquerias usually add fresh salsa, but I don't bother.

NOTE Epazote is a pungent Mexican herb, traditionally used with beans and in quesadillas. It has sawtooth-edged leaves and a strong aroma reminiscent of gasoline or kerosene, but it tastes a lot better than that suggests. Like many herbs, it's expensive to buy but easy to grow. Look for bunches of the herb or small plants in farmers' markets or specialty markets, or ask herb-gardening friends if they have any to spare (it's an annual but reseeds itself easily and often survives the winter here in the San Francisco Bay Area). If you can't find it or don't like it, leave it out.

VARIATION Other good quesadilla fillings (in addition to the basic cheese) include leftover cooked chicken, turkey, or ham or any of the taco fillings on the following pages.

Do-It-Yourself Tacos

■ *Serves 6*

Even the ubiquitous fast-food chains have diversified far beyond "tacos" of crumbly ground beef in crisp fried shells to something more like the original tacos: warm, flexible corn tortillas wrapped around a small amount of meat filling with salsa. It's the classic street food, bought from a storefront taqueria or more often a cart or truck and eaten on the spot.

One of my biggest problems with a lot of taquerias in the United States is the way they pile a lot of filling inside one or two tortillas, making it next to impossible to eat a taco out of hand. Taco trucks tend to be better about this, assuming you will be ordering some number of tacos rather than just one. At the same time, there are some very successful chain restaurants north of the border that have popularized fajitas, which have grown from a single dish (strips of grilled beef skirt steak) to a whole genre, with beef, chicken, or even shrimp served on a sizzling platter with cooked vegetables, beans, rice, and a stack of warm flour tortillas, all ready to assemble to taste.

Still, fajitas wrapped in flour tortillas always leave me a little dissatisfied—it's like having a corned beef sandwich on white bread. Tacos need the earthy taste and texture of corn tortillas. But there's no reason not to adapt the fajita style of serving to tacos, setting out a basket of warm corn tortillas and a buffet of fillings and toppings.

Several options for fillings follow. Other possibilities include Chile Verde (page 172) and Yucatecan Banana-Leaf Pork or Chicken (page 174), either as leftovers or freshly cooked for this use.

Carnitas, Carnitas "al Pastor," or Carne Asada (recipes follow)

2 cups cooked beans (black, pinto, or refried)

1 cup grated or crumbled cheese, preferably a Mexican añejo type like Cotija (page 159); otherwise Jack, Muenster, or mild cheddar

2 cups Salsa Cruda (page 170) or Roasted Tomatillo Sauce (page 181)

OPTIONAL TOPPINGS

Shredded romaine or other crisp lettuce

WHICH BEER?
Anything not too hoppy,
depending on the
heat of your salsa.

Sliced green onion, or minced yellow or white onion rinsed with a little warm water

Chopped cilantro

Poblano or long green chiles, roasted, peeled, and cut into strips

Guacamole

2 dozen 6-inch corn tortillas

Have your choice of meat filling ready and warm. Set out the beans, cheese, salsa, and toppings in individual bowls with spoons. Line a basket or shallow bowl with a decorative cloth towel to receive the tortillas. Warm the tortillas on a griddle or directly over a gas flame until lightly speckled with brown, adding each to the basket before it has a chance to cool.

At the table, spoon a little cheese into a tortilla first (to give it a chance to melt), than add a few bits of meat, some beans, a spoonful of salsa, and your choice of toppings. Fold the tortilla over the filling, bending the other end slightly to hold in the filling as you eat. (Some will drip out anyway; this is short-sleeve food.)

TECHNIQUE NOTE In my multiculturally equipped kitchen, I frequently use Chinese stacking steamer baskets to reheat several items at once, in this case the beans and any leftover meat fillings. I don't use it to warm tortillas, although steaming is pretty standard in taquerias; I much prefer them warmed with dry heat.

Carnitas

■ *Makes about 3 cups*

I know I should expand my horizons when it comes to taco fillings, but I keep coming back to these slightly crunchy "little meats," bits of pork cooked by a uniquely Mexican method that starts with simmering them in water and ends with browning them in their own rendered fat.

2 pounds pork country-style spareribs, or 1½ pounds boneless pork shoulder

½ teaspoon kosher salt

Cut the meat from the bones and trim off the surface fat. Separate the meat along the natural seams, removing excess fat as you find it, and cut into 1- to 2-inch cubes. Place the cubes in a heavy pot that will hold them snugly in a single layer, sprinkle with the salt, and add water just to cover. Bring to a boil, reduce the heat to medium, and cook uncovered at a lively simmer until the meat is tender, 1½ to 2 hours. Periodically skim off any foam that rises to the surface.

Continue cooking until the water evaporates and the meat begins to sizzle in the remaining fat. Turn the cubes so they brown well on all sides, and cook until slightly crisp. Drain and keep warm until ready to chop into shreds for tacos or burritos.

TECHNIQUE NOTE The best tool for chopping carnitas is the one I see used in many Mexican taquerias—a Chinese cleaver. Put a cube on the cutting board, give it a sharp whack with the broad side of the blade so that the meat breaks nearly apart into stringy bits, then chop crosswise. This gives the maximum surface area for salsas to cling to.

Carnitas "al Pastor"

■ *Makes about 3 cups*

This name makes no sense in normal taqueria lingo, as al pastor *(shepherd style) implies meat cooked on a spit and carved off to order. It's a technique that doesn't translate well to small quantities, but the typical chile and vinegar marinade used for meat cooked* al pastor *can be added to carnitas. Meats cooked this way are sometimes called* chilorio, *a version of which used to be on the menu at my favorite Berkeley taqueria but inexplicably disappeared several years ago.*

Any variety of large dried chiles, such as ancho, guajillo, pasilla (negro), California, or New Mexico, will work here; each gives a slightly different flavor, so play around and see which you prefer.

2 pounds pork country-style spareribs, or 1½ pounds boneless pork shoulder

4 or 5 large dried chiles

4 cloves garlic

A little boiling water

$^{1}/_{4}$ **teaspoon peppercorns**

$^{1}/_{8}$ **teaspoon cumin seeds**

2 cloves

$^{1}/_{4}$ **teaspoon dried oregano**

$^{1}/_{3}$ **cup unseasoned rice vinegar or cider vinegar**

$^{1}/_{2}$ **teaspoon kosher salt**

Start the pork cooking as for Carnitas (see the previous recipe). Meanwhile, heat an ungreased skillet or griddle and toast the chiles and garlic. When the chiles are soft and pliable, remove them and set aside for a few seconds to cool, then slit them open with a knife or scissors. Shake out and discard the seeds and remove the ribs. Place the chiles in a small bowl and add boiling water just to cover. Set aside to steep for about an hour.

Toast the garlic, peppercorns, cumin, and cloves on the dry pan until fragrant; add the oregano for a few seconds, then transfer everything to a mortar or blender. If using a mortar, grind the spices and garlic together at your leisure before adding the chile paste (the next step). If using a blender, just leave the whole spices in the machine for now.

When the carnitas are getting close to done, lift the chiles out of the water and carefully scrape the red pulp from the inside with a metal spoon, leaving the outer skin behind. Add this paste to the spices in the mortar or blender, along with the vinegar, salt, and ¼ cup of the chile soaking water, and blend to a paste.

When the meat cubes are beginning to sizzle and brown, remove the meat to a cutting board and add the chile-spice paste to the pan. Shred and chop the meat (see the Technique Note in the Carnitas recipe) and return it to the pan to reheat and coat with the sauce. Taste for seasoning and keep warm until ready to serve.

Carne Asada

▮ *Makes 3 cups*

This is a way of turning relatively lean but tender cuts of beef (the kind that make better roasts than steaks) into quick-cooking, tender, bite-size pieces. Skirt steak used to be a cheap cut for this use, but not since the fajitas craze. If your butcher will slice the meat for you, so much the better.

1¹/₂ to 2 pounds beef sirloin, rump, top round, tri-tip, or chuck "mock tender"

Kosher salt and freshly ground black pepper

Juice of 2 limes

Slice the meat across the grain about ¼ inch thick. If using a small muscle like the mock tender, you can make a continuous strip by cutting almost through to one side, then turning the piece over and cutting parallel to the first cut almost to the edge, repeating the process so it makes a long accordion-folded piece. Pound the slices lightly with a meat pounder, mallet, or the side of a cleaver to thin them slightly, but not so much that the meat falls apart. Season the slices with salt, pepper, and a squeeze of lime juice.

Have a hot grill ready (gas, charcoal, or stovetop). Lay a few meat slices on the grill and cook just until drops of blood appear on top; turn and cook for a few seconds on the other side, then transfer to a warm platter. Repeat with the remaining meat, then chop the slices into bite-size pieces and toss in any juices that have accumulated on the platter.

Salsa Cruda *(Fresh Tomato Salsa)*

▦ *Makes about 1 cup*

1 large or 2 small ripe tomatoes (or 8 ounces oval, Roma-type tomatoes)

Kosher salt

1 small green chile (jalapeño or serrano)

1 good-sized green onion, minced

2 or 3 sprigs cilantro, chopped not too fine

Lime or lemon juice

Split the tomatoes crosswise (lengthwise if using Romas). Holding a half in your palm, gently squeeze and shake out the seeds; discard the seeds. Cut the tomato into medium-fine dice and place in a mixing bowl with a pinch of salt.

Remove the stem end of the chile and split the chile lengthwise. For a milder salsa, carefully cut out the seeds and most of the white ribs; for a hotter flavor, leave them in. Mince the chile finely and add it to the tomato with the green onion and cilantro. Toss to mix well, season to taste with lime juice and more salt if needed, and let stand for half an hour or so before serving.

Festival Time: Oktoberfest, Märzen, Bock, and Other Special Lagers

◼

Before the microbrew revolution, when nearly all North American beer was pale lager, "dark beer" meant a darker-hued version of the same beer, with marginally more flavor than the pale variety. While most of the craft brewing energy in the last quarter century has gone into ales, some new lager breweries looked back to the original Bavarian and Viennese models for darker lagers with more pronounced malty flavor. The most popular model was Munich's Märzenbier (literally "March beer," because it was traditionally brewed in the spring and lagered over the summer to serve at Oktoberfest). What began as a seasonal beer has become a year-round favorite with many beer drinkers, and for good reason. A typical Märzen/Oktoberfest beer is dark amber to reddish brown in color, with medium body, and a rich, malty sweetness in the middle, but usually a dry finish with a good dose of hops. It is a bit higher in alcohol than other lagers but not knockout strong. Overall, it's a style that is easy to enjoy with a variety of foods. I especially like to serve this type of beer with complex, spicy Mexican foods like mole and Yucatecan banana-leaf dishes, not to mention Asian curries, but it's equally at home with German-style sausages or Italian pizza.

By definition, Märzen/Oktoberfest is a lager, and not surprisingly the classic West Coast examples are brewed by lager specialists Gordon Biersch and Sudwerk. However, some ale-brewing microbreweries apply the name to reddish ales with a similar flavor profile.

Bock is another southern German seasonal style, typified by higher-gravity lagers brewed to serve in the spring, the higher alcohol presumably meant to fortify drinkers who can't wait to start the outdoor beer-drinking season. In Germany, bocks come in a whole range of colors, from nearly as pale as Pilsner to doppelbocks nearly as black as stout. While it's not a very common label on the West Coast, bock usually implies a lager that is stronger than the brewery's other lagers, often quite strong (7 percent alcohol by volume or more). Some are presented as winter "-fest" brews rather than spring specialties, which seems appropriate.

Chile Verde

■ *Serves 6 to 8*

The title simple means "green chile pepper," but like "chili" in Texas it can imply a finished dish, in this case pork cooked in a green sauce that actually contains far more tomatillo than chile. North of the border, chile verde is usually a simple meat and sauce dish, popular as a filling for tacos and burritos or served in the middle of a "combination plate" in restaurants. In Mexico it's more likely to be served as a stew with an assortment of vegetables (see Variation).

1 pound fresh tomatillos, peeled and rinsed

1 small onion, peeled and quartered

2 cloves garlic

2 jalapeño or serrano chiles

2 pounds pork country-style spareribs, or 1½ pounds boneless pork shoulder

Kosher salt and freshly ground black pepper

12 sprigs cilantro (optional)

1 cup water

WHICH BEER?

Amber ale, Märzen.

Preheat the broiler. Lay the tomatillos, onions, garlic, and chiles on a shallow baking pan (lined with foil if you like), and broil about 4 inches from the heat, turning once or twice, until well browned, about 15 minutes in all.

Meanwhile, cut the meat into large cubes and trim off most of the fat. Season lightly with salt and pepper. Heat a skillet and grease it with a piece of the fat, then brown the pork cubes a few at a time.

Transfer the broiled vegetables to a blender, add the cilantro and the water, and blend to a rough purée. Add to the skillet when all the meat has been browned. Cover and simmer until the meat is quite tender, about 1¼ hours. If the sauce seems too thin, remove the meat and boil it down a bit before adjusting the seasonings.

To use as a taco filling, remove the meat chunks from the sauce and chop into small pieces, then stir back into the sauce. To serve on a plate, leave the meat in good-sized cubes.

VARIATION To make a more substantial meat-and-vegetable stew, add one or more of the following to the stew for the last 10 to 15 minutes of simmering:

■ Sliced zucchini or other summer squash

■ Cubes of peeled eggplant, salted for 30 minutes, drained, and lightly browned in olive oil

■ Sliced green beans, parboiled until just tender (they should still be slightly "squeaky")

■ Lima beans or fava beans, blanched

■ Diced potatoes (parboiled, or cooked in the stew)

■ Mild green chiles (Anaheim or similar), roasted, peeled, and cut into 1-inch squares

Yucatecan Banana-Leaf Pork or Chicken

■ *Serves 4 to 6*

Cooking meats in a wrapping of banana leaves is not unique to the Yucatán Peninsula; it's done all over the tropics, both as a matter of convenience and for the subtle herbal flavor the leaves give to the food. What gives this dish its Yucatecan flavor is the thick, citrusy marinade based on achiote, a brick-colored seed that is the source of the natural food dye annatto. Achiote seeds are very hard to grind, so I recommend doing as many Yucatecan cooks do and buying it already ground and blended with cumin and other spices. Look for rectangular packages labeled achiote condimentado *in Mexican and Caribbean markets. A blend of citrus juices takes the place of the authentic bitter (Seville) orange, which is available only occasionally in the United States, mainly in winter or early spring.*

By itself, this dish is not especially picante; a few strips of seeded yellow wax chile give just a hint of heat. That's because the table will likely be set with either a fresh or bottled salsa made with the fiery habanero chile.

2 small cloves garlic

¹/₂ teaspoon kosher salt

¹/₂ teaspoon ground cumin

Half a 3.5-ounce cake seasoned ground achiote paste (achiote condimentado)

2 tablespoons orange juice

2 tablespoons lemon or lime juice

A few strips citrus peel, removed with a peeler

1¹/₂ pounds boneless pork shoulder or country-style ribs

3 or 4 yellow wax chiles, or 2 long green chiles

1-pound package frozen banana leaves (sold in Asian and some Latin American groceries), thawed

1 medium red or yellow onion, thinly sliced

WHICH BEER?

A dark, malty Märzen or bock.

Eight to 24 hours ahead of serving, mash the garlic and salt together in a mortar or on the cutting board (see page 191). Combine in a medium bowl with the cumin, achiote paste, and citrus juice and peel, and stir until well blended. Separate the meat along the natural seams, discard the excess fat, and cut larger chunks across the grain into pieces no more than 2 inches thick. Turn the pork cubes in the marinade, cover tightly (or seal in a gallon-size sealable plastic bag), and marinate in the refrigerator.

At your convenience, roast, peel, and seed the chiles and cut the flesh into strips.

Preheat the oven to 250°F, or set up a covered charcoal or gas grill for slow indirect cooking. Remove the pork from the refrigerator. Carefully cut or tear four or six 12-inch squares of banana leaf. Trim off the tough stringy edge (save it for tying the packages, if you like). Rinse the squares with warm water. Lay a square dull side up on the cutting board; cover any tears with a smaller piece of leaf. Pile some onions and chile strips in the center and add a portion of the pork, with its marinade. Folding with the grain, lift two opposite sides of the leaf to meet in the center, then fold this doubled edge over once to form a seam, then fold again to enclose the filling snugly (the "drugstore wrap"). Fold the open ends of the package over the center, the longer one on top, and tie the package shut with strips of leaf or cotton twine. Repeat with the remaining portions.

Bake in a shallow roasting pan, or cook in the covered grill away from the direct heat, until the meat is quite tender when probed with a skewer through the package, about 2 hours. Place the leaf-wrapped packages directly onto individual plates, with scissors for cutting the strings. For a neater presentation, either trim off the ends of each package with scissors or fold the excess back under the middle. Serve with rice or new potatoes.

VARIATION Chicken is equally traditional cooked this way. You can use only legs (my choice) or divide a typical fryer and place half a leg and some breast meat in each package. For big appetites, serve half a chicken, restaurant style. Half a Cornish hen is another option. In any case, chicken cooks somewhat faster than pork, so figure on 1 hour in a 325°F oven.

VARIATION

Banana-Leaf Pork or Chicken en Adobo

If you can't find achiote or don't care for the achiote-based marinade, you can make a more pan-Mexican version based on dried chiles. Omit the achiote paste and roasted chiles in the main recipe. Instead, soak and scrape (see page 158) 3 or 4 smooth dried chiles (in order of increasing heat, California, New Mexico, or guajillo), to yield a scant tablespoon of paste, and combine with the remaining marinade ingredients with an additional $1/2$ teaspoon ground cumin. Marinate, wrap, and bake the meat as described in the main recipe.

Papas a la Huancaína

(Peruvian Potatoes with Cheese Sauce)

■ *Serves 8 as a side dish, 4 as an entrée*

This rib-sticking potato dish with its creamy, chile-spiked sauce strikes me as the Andean equivalent of Alpine fondue or raclette. I first encountered it in an Andean restaurant in Berkeley (long gone) and found this recipe in a book called Totally Hot! Well, a recipe something like this. When I got my copy from one of the authors, food writer Naomi Wise, she had made several changes to the recipe by hand, based on cheeses and other ingredients that had become more common since the book was written but especially because of a revelation that came to her after the book was published: "We were trying to duplicate the texture of the dish at home using fresh milk, but it didn't occur to me until some time later that we had never seen fresh milk during our travels in the Andes. What we did see everywhere was canned evaporated milk." So she retested the recipe with the canned milk, and voilà!

Here, thanks to Naomi, is the updated version, tweaked a bit to my taste. She serves it at room temperature, as a salad with romaine, eggs, and olives. But I prefer it warm, as an appetizer or side dish with simply grilled meats.

¼ cup fresh lemon or lime juice, plus a little more for the sauce

⅛ teaspoon cayenne

Kosher salt

1 small red onion, sliced paper-thin (about 1 cup)

2 pounds new potatoes, red, yellow, or white

1½ ounces (1 cup, loosely packed) slightly stale bread crumbs (about 2 slices, trimmed)

1 small can (8 ounces) evaporated milk

5 ounces Monterey Jack or Muenster cheese, grated

3 ounces mild goat cheese, Mexican-style queso añejo de Cotija, or all-natural cream cheese

¼ cup (or more) mild vegetable oil

1 fresh yellow chile (chile guero or yellow wax chile), seeded and minced (optional)

WHICH BEER?

Anything but the most bitter pale ales or IPA.

6 small dried chiles, seeded and very finely chopped

1 tablespoon chopped garlic

½ cup minced onion

Pinch of dried oregano

Pinch of ground turmeric

1/4 teaspoon kosher salt, or to taste

Freshly ground black pepper

1 egg, beaten

Optional

Lettuce leaves, washed and drained

6 hard-boiled eggs

Kalamata or other black olives, for garnish

Combine ¼ cup lemon juice with a pinch of cayenne and salt to taste. Add the sliced red onion and let stand at room temperature until everything else is ready.

Boil the potatoes in their skins until tender, 20 to 45 minutes, depending on the size. Peel if you like (peeling is traditional in Peru, but optional here).

Combine the bread crumbs with ⅓ cup of the evaporated milk and let them soak until soft. Mix thoroughly with the cheeses. Heat 2 tablespoons oil in a deep, heavy saucepan. Add the fresh and dried chiles and the garlic and sauté briefly to soften. Add the minced onion, oregano, and enough turmeric to give the mixture a golden color. Add salt and pepper to taste (bearing in mind the saltiness of the cheeses, which varies). Cook over medium-low heat until the onion is soft, about 5 minutes. Add the cheese mixture and cook, stirring, until the cheese melts. Remove from the heat and add the raw egg, stirring fiercely. Gradually stir in the remaining evaporated milk, then add oil until the sauce is a little thinner than mayonnaise; finish with a little lemon juice.

To serve warm, slice the potatoes and arrange on a platter or individual plates, spoon the sauce over the slices, and garnishing with well-drained pickled onions. For a salad, let the potatoes and sauce cool to room temperature and serve on a bed of lettuce leaves, topped with the sauce, hard-boiled eggs, olives, and onions.

Empanadas *(Meat-Filled Turnovers)*

■ *Makes 8*

Folded-over meat pies, cousins to British-style pasties, are found all over Mexico through Central America and the Caribbean, under various names (for example, they're called patties in Jamaica). In Spanish-speaking countries, they are generally called empanadas, which simply means something in a crust and can also refer to sweet turnovers. This slightly spicy filling, studded with olives and nuts, is typical of Mexico.

FILLING

³⁄₄ pound ground beef or shredded cooked beef

1¹⁄₂ cups minced onion (1 large)

2 cloves garlic, minced

2 serrano or jalapeño chiles, seeded and minced

10 blanched almonds or 2 tablespoons blanched
  slivered almonds

4 pitted green olives

Heaping tablespoon raisins

Kosher salt and freshly ground black pepper to taste

DOUGH

1¹⁄₂ cups flour

¹⁄₂ teaspoon kosher salt

2 tablespoons cold butter

1 tablespoon cold vegetable shortening, lard, or
  rendered chicken fat (see Note, page 28)

1 egg, beaten

About 3 tablespoons cold water

■

2 tablespoons milk

WHICH BEER?

Because these are more rich than spicy, they go well with pale ale, porter, or stout.

To make the filling, cook the meat in a skillet over low heat until the raw color is gone and the meat begins to brown. (If using cooked meat, cook the rest of the ingredients first in a little oil and add the meat at the end.) Push the meat to one side of the skillet and swab out any excess fat with a paper towel. Add the onion, garlic, and chile and cook until the onion is soft. Meanwhile, coarsely chop the almonds, olives, and raisins. Stir into the cooked meat mixture and season to taste. Let cool.

To make the dough, combine the flour, salt, and fats in a bowl and cut the fat into small pieces. Rub the mixture between your fingertips, breaking up the lumps of fat into small flakes. Stir in the egg (leave a tiny bit behind in the bowl for brushing), then add cold water a tablespoon at a time, stirring with the fingers of one hand, until the dough just comes together. Shape into a ball, wrap tightly, and refrigerate 30 minutes to overnight.

Preheat the oven to 375°F. Divide the dough into 6 even pieces (a scale is handy for this). On a lightly floured surface, roll a piece of dough out to a 7-inch circle, and spoon a scant ¼ cup of the filling on one side. Fold the dough over, press the edges together, then fold about ½ inch of the edge up and inward. Crimp the edges with the times of a fork and transfer to a baking sheet. Repeat with the remaining dough and filling. Add the milk to the bowl with the remaining egg, brush the tops of the pies with a little of the mixture, and make a couple of slits in the tops. Bake until golden brown, about 25 minutes. Serve warm.

Grilled King Salmon with Roasted Tomatillo Sauce

■ *Serves 8*

No, salmon is not a traditional Mexican fish. But it still goes great with a tart, spicy sauce based on Mexican tomatillos. This is equally good with other wild Pacific salmon, including coho, sockeye, and top-quality chum, or "silver-bright." For that matter, it tastes great with California halibut, mahi-mahi, grouper, or various other fish that really do come from Mexican waters. The sauce also works well as a salsa for tacos, quesadillas, and the like, or just as a dip for tortilla chips.

The Summer Vegetable "Napoleon" on page 87 isn't particularly Latin either, but it looks and tastes great with this dish.

TOMATILLO SAUCE

2$\frac{1}{2}$ pounds fresh tomatillos, peeled and rinsed

1 tablespoon olive oil

2 cloves garlic, minced

2 green onions, sliced

1 or 2 small green chiles, seeded and minced

$\frac{1}{4}$ cup chopped cilantro

$\frac{1}{2}$ teaspoon kosher salt, or to taste

■

3 pounds king salmon fillet

Kosher salt and freshly ground black pepper

WHICH BEER?

Hefeweizen or Pilsner.

Rub the tomatillos with a little oil and roast in a hot oven under a broiler, or directly on the grill until the skins are blistered and beginning to burst. Transfer to a blender or food processor and blend to a slightly chunky purée. Heat the oil in a medium saucepan and cook the garlic, green onion, and chiles for a couple of minutes without browning. Add the tomatillo purée and cilantro, cook until slightly thickened, and season to taste with salt.

Prepare a medium-hot fire in a charcoal or gas grill. Slice the salmon on the diagonal into 8 equal pieces about ½ inch thick (or have it cut at the fish market). Season the slices lightly on both sides with salt and pepper.

Grill the salmon, starting on the bone side and turning once, until a skewer inserted into the thickest part comes out warm, about 2 minutes per side. Meanwhile, spread the tomatillo sauce on warm plates and place a wedge of the vegetable terrine (if serving) on each. Add the salmon, bone side up, and serve immediately.

VARIATION You can cook the salmon by whatever method is most convenient—grilling, broiling, on a stovetop grill, or simply baking it uncovered on a lightly oiled pan in a hot oven. While you're at it, use the same heat source to roast the tomatillos.

Sweet Corn Chowder with Chipotle Butter

■ *Serves 8*

Just a dab of smoky chipotle takes this simple soup to a new level and reminds us of how much European cuisines were enriched by these three foods from the New World—corn, potatoes, and chiles.

4 ears sweet corn (white, yellow, or both)

2 medium onions, 1 finely diced and 1 quartered

About 6 cups water or mild (unsalted) chicken stock

1 teaspoon kosher salt

3½ tablespoons unsalted butter

1 canned chipotle chile en adobo

2 medium baking potatoes, peeled and finely diced

2 cups milk

Freshly ground white pepper to taste

WHICH BEER?
I don't see this soup as having a special beer match of its own; just serve whatever you'll be drinking with the course that follows.

Husk the corn and remove the silk. Cut the kernels from the cobs into a bowl, cutting off about the top half of each. Scrape the cobs with the back of the knife blade to force out the hearts of the kernels. Combine the scraped cobs in a stockpot with the quartered onion and water or stock just to cover. Add 1 teaspoon salt, bring to a boil, reduce the heat to low, cover, and simmer 30 minutes. Remove from the heat.

While the stock simmers, set 2 tablespoons of the butter in a bowl in a warm place to soften (but not melt). Slit open the chile (if a little of the adobo stays attached, that's fine) and force it through a fine sieve into the bowl with the butter. Beat with a pinch of salt until well combined; cover and set aside.

Melt the remaining 1½ tablespoons butter in a soup pot over low heat. Add the diced onion and cook until it begins to soften. Add the potatoes and strain in the corn stock. Bring to a simmer and cook 15 minutes, then add the corn and cook another 15 minutes, or until the potatoes and corn are tender. Add the milk, season to taste with salt and pepper, and simmer just until heated through; do not let it boil after this point or the milk may curdle. Serve with a dollop of chipotle butter in each bowl.

Fish with Ancho Chile Paste and Cream

■ *Serves 4*

This dish uses a little ancho chile paste (see page 158) as a marinade for fish, with more mixed with lightly sour Mexican-style cream for a sauce. It works best on relatively lean, white fish like California halibut, white seabass (the local fish, not the oily Chilean version), or the best grades of rockfish, but you can also use it on salmon if you don't mind the color of the sauce almost matching the color of the fish.

Steamed or roasted new potatoes make a good side dish; if roasting, you might as well use the same oven to cook the fish.

WHICH BEER?

As with other creamy dishes, I find myself reaching for the porter, either regular or smoked.

2 dried ancho chiles (often labeled "chile pasilla" in California)

4 fillet portions halibut, fancy rockfish, white seabass, or salmon, 4 to 7 ounces each

Kosher salt and freshly ground black pepper

½ cup crème fraîche (see Note) or Mexican-style cream

1 tablespoon oil

One and a half to 24 hours ahead of cooking, slit the chiles open with a knife or scissors and discard the stems, seeds, and as much of the ribs as you can remove. Place the chiles in a small bowl, add boiling water just to cover, and soak 1 hour to overnight.

Drain the soaked chiles and lay them out flat on a plate. Carefully scrape the pulp from the inside surface with a spoon until only the translucent skin remains. Discard the skins.

Season the fish portions with salt and a little pepper. Rub about a third of the chile paste on the fish and set aside for 30 minutes. Combine the remaining chile paste with the cream and a pinch of salt and set aside in a warm place.

Heat the oil in a large skillet (preferably nonstick) over medium heat. Add the fish, bone side down, and cook until the chile paste begins to brown. Turn and cook on the other side until a skewer inserted into the thickest part of the fish comes out warm. Alternatively, lay the fish portions face up on a rimmed baking sheet and bake in a preheated 400°F oven until done by the skewer test. Either way, the total cooking time will be 6 to 10 minutes, depending on the variety and thickness of the fish.

Warm the chile cream gently in a small saucepan while the fish cooks. Transfer the fish portions face up to warm plates or a serving platter, spoon the sauce over and around the fish, and serve immediately.

NOTE Many Mexican markets carry jars of cultured cream, very similar to French-style crème fraîche. Both are less sour and less thick than typical American sour cream, and behave better in cooking. Far cheaper than buying either one is to make your own: Warm ½ pint whipping cream (look for the natural form, not ultrapasteurized and without any additives) to 100°F in a double boiler. Remove from the heat and stir in 1 tablespoon cultured buttermilk. Transfer to a clean glass jar, cover, and let stand in a warm spot overnight, then refrigerate. It takes a couple of days to reach its full thickness, and will keep for about two weeks.

BEER IN THE MELTING POT:

Beer and American Regional Food

Wander all over the country tasting regional favorites—crab cakes in Maryland, barbecue in the Carolinas, chili in Texas, étouffée or court-bouillon in Louisiana, clambake in New England, or chimichangas in Arizona—and chances are you will be offered a beer along with your meal. The same goes for the newest fusion cuisines, whether they go under labels like East-West, Pacific Rim, or whatever. And these days, the beer is as likely to be a local or regional craft brew as a national brand.

Here are some of my favorites from this regional bounty, as well as some all-American favorites like meat loaf and that homebrewer's standby, beer bread—all of them good partners to West Coast craft-brewed beers.

Spicy Chicken Wings

■ *Makes 24 pieces*

The most famous chicken-wing snack in America is "Buffalo wings," which come not from bison but from a bar in Buffalo, New York. Authentic Buffalo wings combine a spicy marinade, blue cheese dressing for dipping, and celery sticks. These are not those, just a simple way to present chicken wing sections as zingy, have-another-sip-of-beer appetizers.

The technique of partially boning the wing sections into tiny drumstick shapes is optional but makes for less messy eating. If you don't want to bother and have plenty of napkins, just cut the wings apart at the joints and discard the tips.

WHICH BEER?

You name it, with the usual caveat about very hoppy beers and very spicy foods.

1 dozen chicken wings

1 tablespoon kosher salt

¼ teaspoon dried thyme

¼ teaspoon dry mustard

¼ teaspoon sweet paprika

⅛ to ¼ teaspoon cayenne

⅛ teaspoon ground white pepper

1 tablespoon oil

Divide the wings at the first (elbow) joint. Cut away any excess skin and fat. For the upper pieces, cut the meat and skin free from the bone at the smaller end, and scrape and push the meat halfway up toward the large end. For the middle sections, cut all around about ¼ inch above the upper joint, cutting through skin and tendon, and cut between the two bones where they meet at the other (open) end. Bend the wing tip backwards until one of the two bones comes free; push this bone out one end or the other, then cut off and discard the wing tip. Loosen the meat and skin from one end of the remaining bone and push the meat toward one end. You should have 24 pieces, each with a bit of protruding bone to serve as a handle.

Combine the salt, thyme, and spices and sprinkle over the wing pieces in a bowl. Add the oil and toss to coat evenly. Marinate for a few minutes to several hours.

Preheat the oven to 375°F. Spread the wing pieces in a shallow baking dish and bake 35 minutes, or until the juices run clear. Serve hot or warm.

Crab Cakes with Chipotle Aioli

■ *Serves 4 to 8*

East Coast, Gulf Coast, West Coast, or anywhere in between, one of the favorite things to do with crabmeat is make it into crisp crab cakes. Whether you use our local Dungeness crab or crab imported from elsewhere, crab cakes should be mostly about crabmeat, with just enough other stuff to hold them together and provide a complimentary flavor. If serving them with a spicy sauce like the one here, you can keep the crab cake seasonings simple. One cake makes a nice addition to a salad course, two a light entrée.

1 pound crabmeat

1 egg

2 tablespoons mayonnaise

2 teaspoons Worcestershire sauce

1 teaspoon prepared mustard

$\frac{1}{2}$ teaspoon kosher salt, plus more for dressing

$\frac{1}{2}$ teaspoon paprika

$\frac{1}{4}$ teaspoon freshly ground black pepper, plus more for dressing

$\frac{1}{4}$ cup dry bread crumbs

1 tablespoon chopped parsley or cilantro

Oil, for pan-frying

2 teaspoons vinegar

3 tablespoons olive oil

3 to 4 cups mixed salad greens

Chipotle Aioli (recipe follows)

WHICH BEER?

Pale ale hefeweizen, Pilsner.

Look over the crabmeat and remove any bits of shell. Combine with the egg, mayonnaise, Worcestershire, mustard, salt, paprika, pepper, bread crumbs, and parsley and mix gently with a fork until everything is evenly moistened but some good-sized chunks of crab remain. (A two-tined cook's fork makes a good tool for combining the ingredients without breaking up the crab too much.) Refrigerate until ready to cook.

Generously coat a 12-inch skillet with oil and set it over medium heat. For each cake, scoop up about ⅓ cup of the crab mixture and gently form it into a thick patty. Cook until nicely browned on both sides and heated through, 3 to 5 minutes per side, depending on the thickness. While the cakes cook, combine the vinegar in a salad bowl with a pinch of salt and pepper to taste, stir to dissolve the salt, then stir in the olive oil. Taste on a lettuce leaf and adjust the seasonings. Toss the salad in this dressing and arrange on plates. Top each salad with 1 or 2 crab cakes, and either add a generous spoonful of Chipotle Aioli to each plate or drizzle it over all with a squeeze bottle.

Chipotle Aioli

■ *Makes ⅔ cup*

A little bit of chipotle chile, the ripened and smoke-dried form of the jalapeño, gives a lot of chile zing to the garlic mayonnaise of Provence. Include a little of the adobo, the vinegar-based paste found in the can with the chiles.

3 cloves garlic

½ teaspoon kosher salt

2 egg yolks

1 canned chipotle chile, minced

1 teaspoon adobo from the chile can

About ½ cup mild olive oil

1 teaspoon mild vinegar, or to taste

Pound the garlic and salt together to a smooth paste in a mortar (or mash repeatedly with the broad side of a knife on an impervious surface). Scrape into a mixing bowl, add the egg yolks, chile, and adobo, and beat with a whisk to a paler shade of yellow. Add a spoonful of the oil and beat until it is absorbed. Continue adding oil in small quantities, beating constantly, until the sauce forms a smooth emulsion. After about ¼ cup oil has been added, alternate oil and a few drops of vinegar, until the sauce is nice and thick. Taste and correct the seasoning. Strain through a fine sieve before serving.

VARIATION For plain aioli, leave out the chipotle. For a brightly colored saffron aioli, crush a large pinch of saffron threads with the garlic.

Warm Escarole Salad with Smoked Chicken

▓ *Serves 4 as a first course, 2 as an entrée*

This can serve as a basic model for warm salad: some greens on the bitter side, a small amount of flavorful meat or poultry, a splash of vinegar and some warm oil, and perhaps some other vegetables or nuts, all adding up to a salad that is substantial enough to serve as a lunch or dinner entrée. The smoked chickens sold in delis are convenient and tasty, if a bit pricey; of course, if you smoke your own chicken (or turkey or duck) you will save some money.

Scant cup smoked chicken meat, with or without skin

3 tablespoons olive oil

1 cup julienned red or yellow onion

1 red or yellow bell pepper, seeded and sliced (optional)

1 tablespoon vinegar

$\frac{1}{2}$ teaspoon kosher salt

$\frac{1}{4}$ teaspoon freshly ground black pepper, or to taste

1 small head escarole or curly endive, torn, washed, and spun dry (about 4 cups torn greens)

WHICH BEER?

Pale ale or amber ale.

Cut the chicken into bite-size strips, removing the skin or leaving it on as you prefer. Heat the oil over medium heat in a skillet and cook the onions and peppers until tender. Meanwhile, combine the vinegar, salt, and pepper in a stainless steel or other heatproof bowl, and stir with your fingertips to dissolve the salt. Add the greens and toss with the seasoned vinegar.

When the onions and peppers are ready, add the chicken to the pan just to heat it through, then pour the contents of the skillet over the greens; use a handful of greens to swab out the last of the oil in the skillet. Toss quickly, then arrange the greens on plates, topping with the other ingredients.

NOTE If your greens are on the tough side, as escarole and larger curly endive can be, you can cook them for a few seconds in the pan rather than simply wilting them with the hot oil. Use an extra-large skillet, wok, or stir-fry pan to provide enough room to toss the greens in the hot dressing.

VARIATIONS The warm salad theme lends itself to endless variations. Here are a few:

▨ Substitute arugula for some or all of the greens, or use a braising mix (prewashed small greens that look superficially similar to a mesclun-style salad mix but are heavier on the sturdy and bitter varieties).

▨ Scrape most of the fat off 1 or 2 legs of chicken or duck confit (page 75) and reheat the confit in a steamer or double boiler. Use a little less oil for sautéing the onions and peppers, and add the fatty drippings from the reheated confit to the skillet along with the sliced meat.

▨ Cook sliced pancetta, bacon, or your favorite sausage first in the skillet (fully cooked sausages just need to be reheated and browned slightly); then either use the drippings from the meat or discard them and replace them with olive oil.

▨ Omit the red pepper and garnish the salad with pomegranate seeds or bits of tart dried fruit like cranberries, cherries, or apricots, plumped in a little warm water if they are too dry to enjoy on their own.

Grilled Salmon Sandwich

■ *Serves 4*

After burgers, fish and chips, and Caesar salad, probably the most ubiquitous item on West Coast brewpub menus is a sandwich made with a smallish portion of grilled salmon. Like any other dish, it's only as good as its basic ingredients: salmon, bread, greens, and sauce.

Most kitchens simply use farm-raised Atlantic salmon, which is available all year, consistent in size, and fatty enough that it is moist even if overcooked, as it often is. For the best sandwich, however, seek out wild king (chinook) or sockeye salmon, fresh in season or frozen the rest of the year.

My first choice for bread would be a crusty, slightly sour loaf made with some whole wheat or rye flour, such as Acme Upstairs Bread from Berkeley. Use mild lettuce or a more bitter-peppery green like arugula, as you prefer. I like the garlicky flavor of aioli with grilled salmon, but feel free to use tartar sauce, basil-flavored mayonnaise (see Grilled Eggplant Sandwich, page 198), or any other doctored-mayo sauce you like.

WHICH BEER?
I go back and forth between hefeweizen and pale ale with this, depending on my mood and the weather.

1 pound salmon fillet, skin and pin bones removed

Kosher salt and freshly ground black pepper

8 slices crusty bread, lightly toasted

¼ cup plain or saffron-flavored aioli (see Variation, page 191), or ¼ cup mayonnaise mixed with 1 teaspoon chopped capers

Red-leaf or other tender lettuce leaves, or a handful of arugula leaves

Slice the salmon diagonally into 8 thin cutlets about 2 ounces each. Season with a little salt and pepper. Grill over a hot fire, broil, or sear in a nonstick skillet until just done, 2 to 3 minutes per side. Meanwhile, spread the bread with aioli and top half the slices with lettuce. Put 2 slices of salmon on each sandwich and serve immediately.

VARIATION Tuck some pickled onion rings (see Papas a la Huancaína, page 177) into the sandwiches.

NOTE If all you can find are salmon steaks rather than fillets, choose 2 large ones (9 to 10 ounces each) and divide them as follows: Locate the central bone, the ribs splitting off around the belly cavity, and the bones extending up toward the dorsal fin opposite the ribs. With a short, stiff knife, cut through the ribs where they join the central bone, leaving them attached to the meat. Cut as close as possible to the central bone to free all the meat from one side of the steak, and repeat on the other side. You now have two thick fillet sections with skin and ribs attached. Slip the knife under the ribs to separate them from the meat, and trim off the last ½ inch or so of belly flap. Holding a piece skin side down against the cutting board, scrape the knife against the skin at about a 20-degree angle to "shave" the meat away from the skin. Find the tips of the pin bones running diagonally through the thickest part of the meat and pull them out with tweezers or clean needle-nose pliers. Finally, divide each fillet section in half horizontally, yielding 8 identical portions.

Drink Your Wheaties:
Hefeweizen and Other Wheat Beers

■

Most beer (other than some made with adjuncts like corn and rice) is made from barley malt, but some regions of northern Europe have a tradition of brewing pale-colored beers with wheat (malted or not) making up half or more of the grain. Local practices, water, climate, and above all yeast strains have yielded several distinctive local styles, from the tart Berliner *weisse* of northern Germany to the baffling variety of Belgian wit, lambic, and gueuze styles and the clove-smelling weizen-bier of Bavaria. Drawing on these Old World models but not precisely matching any of them, many West Coast ale brewers have added a wheat beer or two to their product line. Some use a variant of the word *weiss,* German for "white," others the similar-sounding but unrelated *weizen* ("wheat").

The most common style and label for West Coast wheat beers is hefeweizen, a Bavarian term that means the beer is bottled or packaged in kegs without a final filtration. The spent yeast remaining in the beer adds flavor and is intended to wind up in the glass. Most ale brewers now offer a hefeweizen, some only as a summer seasonal brew, others all year. They vary widely in flavor and especially in the prominence of the hops. Some are very tasty brew; however, despite their use of Bavarian yeast strains, I have yet to taste a domestic hefeweizen with more than a slight suggestion of the distinctive phenolic-clove aroma of the Bavarian model.

An intriguing alternative that is gaining in popularity with western brewers is Belgian wit (which means simply "white"), an especially pale wheat beer flavored with coriander seed and orange peel in addition to hops. (Interestingly, most brewers who feature Belgian styles proudly say so on the label, but Humboldt Hefeweizen, one of my favorite West Coast wheats, mentions the coriander and orange only on its Web site, not on its label.)

While there may be little consensus as to what a West Coast wheat beer should taste like, there is no question that it is a popular style. For many ale breweries and brewpubs, hefeweizen has become their "Pilsner"—the lightest and least bitter beer on the list and often one of the most popular. And it is almost invariably served with a wedge of lemon, Bavarian style. To my taste, some hefes are improved by a squeeze of lemon, others are not, so taste before you add.

Maybe it's just a lingering association with the tart, lactic-acid wheat beers of northern Germany and Belgium, or maybe it's the pale color suggesting a white wine, or maybe it's just that squeeze of lemon, but I often think of wheat beer with seafood, both to drink and occasionally to cook with (see Mussels Steamed in Wheat Beer, page 23). And when having a multicourse meal with several beers, I often choose a hefeweizen with the appetizers and then move on to a fuller-bodied beer later on.

Grilled Eggplant Sandwich

■ *Serves 4*

Here is the vegetarian counterpart of the grilled salmon sandwich, and it's just as popular with brewpub diners.

WHICH BEER?

Pale ale.

12 leaves fresh basil

Pinch of kosher salt

2 tablespoons mayonnaise

3 tablespoons olive oil

1 clove garlic, crushed

8 ounces mozzarella, preferably fresh fior di latte style

1½ pounds small or medium eggplant

Salt and freshly ground black pepper

8 slices crusty bread

Tear the basil leaves into small pieces and place in a bowl or mortar with a pinch of salt. Mash with the back of a spoon or a pestle until nearly liquefied. Stir in the mayonnaise and let stand for an hour or so to allow the flavors to blend. Combine the olive oil and garlic and set aside. Slice the cheese across the grain and leave it out of the refrigerator for at least 20 minutes before assembling the sandwiches.

Slice the eggplant crosswise about ¼ inch thick and sprinkle with a little salt and pepper. Grill over a moderately hot fire (or broil about 3 inches from a preheated broiler), basting with the garlic-flavored oil after each turn, until tender and nicely browned. Remove from the heat and top each slice with mozzarella. Toast the bread slices on the same fire, then spread a little basil mayonnaise on one or both slices before making the sandwiches.

VARIATIONS

■ Sliced tomatoes always go well with eggplant, mozzarella, and basil.

■ Try aioli (see the variation on page 191) in place of the basil mayonnaise.

Fish Baked in Beer Batter

■ *Serves 4*

Baking fish fillets in a very hot oven under a soufflé-like puff of beer-scented batter keeps them especially moist. The high oven temperature is required to get the topping to brown in the short time it takes to cook the fish. A thin but flavorful red pepper sauce binds the fish, topping, and spinach garnish together.

This technique will work with fillets of just about any mild, white fish (flounder, sole, tilapia, rockfish, cod, or halibut), as well as with fuller-flavored fish like salmon and striped bass. Just make sure the fish is cut no more than ³/₄ inch thick or it may not cook by the time the batter is browning.

1 pound fish fillets, no more than ³/₄ inch thick

³/₄ teaspoon kosher salt

Freshly ground white pepper

¹/₂ cup all-purpose flour, plus extra for dusting fillets

²/₃ cup roasted and peeled red pepper or pimiento (about 1 large)

¹/₃ cup unsalted chicken stock

1 tablespoon extra virgin olive oil

1 egg yolk, beaten

¹/₂ cup beer (any type)

1 tablespoon mild olive oil

2 egg whites

12 ounces fresh spinach leaves

WHICH BEER?
Pale ale, hefeweizen, or pale lager; a dry finish is what's important here.

Preheat the oven to 500°F. Rinse the fish fillets and pat dry. Cut into 4 equal portions. Season with ¼ teaspoon salt and a pinch of pepper. Dust the top of the fish with flour and shake off the excess. Coat a shallow 2-quart baking dish lightly with oil or cooking spray and lay in the fish portions 1 inch apart.

For the sauce, purée the peppers, stock, and extra virgin olive oil in a blender or food processor. Keep warm.

Combine the egg yolk, beer, mild olive oil, ½ teaspoon salt, and a pinch of pepper in a bowl and stir to dissolve the salt. Gradually add ½ cup flour and stir with a whisk until smooth. Beat the egg whites in another bowl to soft peaks and fold into the batter. Spoon the batter over the fish and bake until the batter is puffed and golden brown and the fish is tender when probed with a skewer, 8 to 12 minutes, depending on the type and thickness of the fish. Meanwhile, steam the spinach until wilted; keep warm. To serve, cut between the fish and lift out the portions with a large spatula. Spoon the red pepper sauce around the fish and arrange the spinach on top of the sauce, using spinach to disguise any ragged edges of the batter.

VARIATION For the neatest presentation, top and bake each portion of fish in an individual shallow casserole and serve in the baking dish, with the spinach on the side and the sauce spooned over the fish. In this case, reduce the baking time by a minute or two, as the fish will continue to cook from the heat absorbed by the baking dish.

Chili, My Way

■ *Serves 6*

One could write a whole book—in fact, I'm sure many books have been writ-ten—on the subject of chili, and how the Mexican carne con chile colorado *("meat with red chile sauce"), evolved into the archetypal Tex-Mex dish* chili con carne, *now available in cans in every supermarket in America. I can't think of another dish that has spawned so many variations, with every imaginable meat and variety of chile, with tomatoes and bell peppers, with or without beans, and vegetarian versions. Not to mention serving it as a topping for hamburgers and hot dogs, and even over spaghetti (Cincinnati style).*

Everyone who has ever eaten or cooked chili has some idea of what it is supposed to be—now I'm going to tell you mine. First of all, it's a meat dish. You can make a tasty stew of beans and vegetables, but please don't call it chili. Second, it should be made with dried red chiles and selected spices, not some preblended "chili powder." I like to use a north-of-the-border chile like the long, smooth, mild-to-medium California chile or its slightly hotter New Mexico cousin. But if you want to use ancho, guajillo, or another Mexican variety, be my guest. Third, I like the meat chopped, not ground.

And on the all-important question of beans or not? To tell the truth, I like it both ways. Sometimes I stir beans into the chili, sometimes I serve them on the side, sometimes I serve it without beans. As for the type of beans, pintos are classic, and black beans, once trendy, are now standard in much of the West. My favorite, however, is the pinquito, the "little pink" bean that is like a smaller pinto, and I also like the small red bean used in New Orleans red beans and rice. Kidney beans are far too big and beany for my taste, plus they are the wrong color.

What to serve with chili? I grew up on canned chili with beans, topped with grated cheese and shredded lettuce (Mom and Dad added chopped raw onion) and corn chips (Fritos, to be precise) on the side. My own family likes cornbread with chili. I'm happiest with warm corn tortillas.

WHICH BEER?

Märzen or a not-too-hoppy
amber ale.

1 beef chuck roast, blade or 7-bone, 2 to 3 pounds

1 teaspoon kosher salt, or to taste

2 cups water

6 to 8 whole dried California or New Mexico chile pods

Scant teaspoon cumin seeds

½ teaspoon peppercorns

1 tablespoon coriander seeds

1 large onion, diced

2 cloves garlic, minced

½ teaspoon dried oregano

2 cups cooked beans (black, pinquito, small red, or pinto; optional)

Separate the roast along the natural seams and remove the large pieces of fat. Bone out the flatiron (see page 82) and keep it separate for another use, if you like. Heat a large, deep skillet or Dutch oven over medium-low heat and rub it with a bit of the fat to grease it lightly. Season the meat with a little of the salt and brown well on both sides. Add the water, plus the bones if you have no better use for them; cover the pan, and adjust the heat to a low simmer.

While the meat cooks, heat a small dry skillet and toast the chiles until pliable but not scorched. Remove from the pan and cut off the stem ends with scissors. Shake out the seeds and pull out as much of the ribs as you can (you can do this with the scissors to avoid getting chile oil on your fingers). Cut the chiles into 1-inch pieces and add them to the pot with the meat and water. Toast the whole spices in the same pan until fragrant, and transfer to a mortar or spice grinder; grind at your leisure.

Cook the meat covered, on top of the stove or in a 250°F oven, until quite tender, about 2 hours. Transfer the meat to a plate and strain the contents of the pot into a heatproof container. Let the broth stand until the fat rises to the top, then ladle 2 tablespoons of the fat back into the pot. Add the onions, garlic, ground spices, and oregano and cook over low heat until the onion is translucent. Meanwhile, pick out the chile pieces from the strainer and the meat platter and place in a blender. Discard the remaining fat from the broth. Transfer the cooked onions and other contents of the pot to the blender and add enough of the broth to facilitate blending. Blend to a smooth paste and pour it back into the pot. Use the remaining broth to rinse out the blender jar and add it to the pot. Add the remaining salt and bring to a simmer.

Chop the meat coarsely with a large knife or cleaver, discarding the bones and any visible fat. Add to the pot to reheat in the sauce. Correct the seasoning and serve with or without beans.

TECHNIQUE NOTE Most of the heat in chiles is in the ribs and tissues carrying the seeds, so if you want a milder chile, take care to remove as much of the ribs as you can. On the other hand, if you want it hotter, leave them in.

NOTE If you can find pure ground California or New Mexico chile powder that is reasonably fresh (in a Mexican market or another place where the stock turns over quickly), you can skip toasting and cutting up the chiles and add 2 tablespoons of the powder to cook with the meat. In this case, you can also skip the step of puréeing the sauce, which is mostly about grinding up the chiles.

Cheese and Beer Bread

■ *Makes 1 loaf*

Beer breads are among the most popular and commonly shared recipes in the homebrewing world. I suspect there are two main reasons for this: Baking and brewing are somewhat similar processes of following recipes and tinkering with them, and homebrewers usually have lots of beer on hand to experiment with. But you don't have to use homemade beer; just about any bottled beer will work for this slightly sweet, muffinlike tea bread, though a really hoppy ale might be too much. In any case, expect the beer aroma to take a while to emerge as the bread cools and to peak in about 24 hours.

WHICH BEER?
Whatever goes with the rest of the menu.

2 cups all-purpose flour

³/₄ cup plus 2 tablespoons whole wheat flour

1 tablespoon baking powder

Scant teaspoon kosher salt

¹/₄ cup sugar

2 ounces grated sharp cheddar (about 1 cup)

2 eggs, beaten

3 tablespoons corn oil

1 tablespoon prepared spicy brown mustard

1¹/₄ cups beer (any type)

Preheat the oven to 350°F. Coat a 9- by 5-inch loaf pan with cooking spray.

Sift the dry ingredients together into a medium bowl. Stir in the cheese. Beat the eggs, oil, and mustard together in a small bowl and add to the dry ingredients along with the beer. Stir just until the dry ingredients are evenly moistened. Spread evenly in the loaf pan and bake until a toothpick or cake tester inserted in the center comes out clean, 40 to 45 minutes. Let cool 15 minutes in the pan, then turn out and cool on a wire rack. Serve at room temperature.

VARIATION

■ Omit the mustard and add a teaspoon of curry powder to the dry ingredients. The curry flavor in the finished bread will be barely detectable, but it supports the other flavors nicely.

Meat Loaf

■ *Serves 6*

Is there any more comforting all-American comfort food than meat loaf? If you don't already have a recipe for meat loaf, here's a good one. You can make it with straight ground beef, but I find a combination of meats more interesting. Serve with your choice of mashed potatoes or Roasted Potato Wedges (recipe follows) and your favorite condiment.

Diners usually serve meat loaf with gravy, but when I was growing up we kids usually had ketchup, and Mom and Dad used "chili sauce" (basically a chunkier, slightly spicier version of ketchup). Sometimes Mom would put some chili sauce into the meatloaf itself. Today, I'm most likely to reach for the mustard.

2½ pounds ground meat (beef, pork, turkey, veal, or a combination)

2 eggs

¼ cup dry bread crumbs

½ teaspoon kosher salt

½ teaspoon garlic salt

½ teaspoon freshly ground black pepper, or to taste

1 teaspoon Worcestershire sauce

1 tablespoon prepared mustard

WHICH BEER?

In case you haven't figured it out by now, pale ale is my default choice with a lot of foods. What's yours?

Preheat the oven to 350°F. Put all the ingredients into a bowl and mix well by hand or with the paddle attachment of a stand mixer. If you want to check the seasoning, pinch off a small piece and cook it in a skillet until it loses its raw color; adjust the seasonings as necessary.

Press the meat mixture into a 9- by 5-inch loaf pan, or shape into a compact oval in a 9- by 13-inch or larger baking dish (see Technique Note). Bake to an internal temperature of 140°F, 50 to 60 minutes depending on the shape and the type of pan. At this stage the center will still be a little pink; if you prefer it cooked more, bake to 145° to 150°F. Any higher and it may come out too dry and crumbly.

Hold the loaf in place with a large spatula and drain away the fat and juices before transferring the loaf to a cutting board. Let the loaf rest for a few minutes before slicing.

TECHNIQUE NOTE I have always baked meat loaf in a loaf pan, so I was surprised the first time I saw my wife make one as a freestanding loaf baked in a larger roasting pan. Her way doesn't make for neat rectangular slices, but it allows more of the fat to drain away. As long as you don't overcook it, either method works fine.

Roasted Potato Wedges

■ *Serves 6*

3 pounds good-sized potatoes (Yukon Gold, Yellow Finn, or russet)

1/2 teaspoon kosher salt

Freshly ground black pepper to taste

1 to 2 tablespoons olive oil

Scrub the potatoes well, but do not peel. Halve lengthwise and cut each half into 3 or 4 wedges. Place them in a shallow roasting pan, sprinkle with salt and pepper, and drizzle with olive oil. Turn to coat on all sides with the oil, then set them skin sides down. Roast at whatever temperature the other dishes you're making call for, anywhere from 325° to 450°F, until tender inside and crisp and golden outside, 25 to 45 minutes depending on size and temperature. If you have to remove them from the oven before the other dishes are ready, keep them warm on top of the stove or return them to the oven briefly to reheat just before serving.

Perfect Roast Chicken

◼ *Serves 3 to 4*

To paraphrase Barbara Kafka in her book Roasting: A Simple Art, *when in doubt, roast a chicken. When you are too tired to think of what else to cook, roast a chicken. When you want to entertain someone special, roast a chicken. When you want to taste a special bottle with dinner, roast a chicken. Like the host with impeccable manners who makes everyone else around him feel like the guest of honor, a good, simply roasted chicken shows any beverage—beer, wine, iced tea, or Kool-Aid—in the best possible light. Add some Roasted Potato Wedges (see opposite) or Garlic Mashed Potatoes (page 209), a salad or some frozen peas, and a baguette for a simply great meal.*

After all the mixed advice I have read and tried—roasting upside down, turning, trussed or not, hot or moderate oven temperature, I have found a method that works every time, without trussing or turning. Brine (see page 208) is a big part of it; this is the same brine I use in a larger batch for the Thanksgiving turkey (see page 226). Of course, you have to have a good, tasty chicken. You may have to go to a butcher shop or a specialty market to find locally and naturally raised birds, but it's worth the trip and the slight extra cost.

See the carving tips for turkey; chicken has all the same parts, just smaller.

BRINE

8 cups water

⅓ cup kosher salt

½ cup apple juice, fresh or from frozen concentrate

1 bay leaf

1 sprig thyme

½ teaspoon peppercorns

◼

1 large fryer or roasting chicken, 3½ to 5 pounds

WHICH BEER?

The best beer you can obtain or the most familiar and basic—it'll taste good with this.

Combine the brine ingredients in a large bowl or pitcher, stirring to dissolve the salt. Place the chicken in a strong, food-grade plastic bag (see Note), pour in the brine, and gather up the bag to surround the chicken and expel all the air. Seal the bag with a twist tie and refrigerate in a bowl 6 hours to overnight. Drain, rinse, and pat dry before roasting.

Preheat the oven to 375°F. Roast the chicken breast side up, without trussing, legs facing toward the back of the oven, to an internal temperature of 160°F in the breast and thigh, 50 minutes to 1 hour and 10 minutes. Let rest 10 to 20 minutes before carving on a cutting board that will catch the juices.

Brining Meats for Moisture and Flavor

For centuries, processors have used curing in brine as a step in many preserved meat products, from corned beef and ham to smoked salmon. Somewhere along the line, someone realized that brine can have a beneficial effect on many everyday meat and poultry dishes, and the idea has spread like wildfire in the last few years, through professional food conferences, newspaper food sections, magazines, cooking classes, and individual recipe swapping.

I have become a great believer in brining, and use it in a number of recipes in this book. In a way, brining goes against intuition. If you look at raw meat soaked in a salt and/or sugar solution as a classic experiment in osmosis, then water should be drawn out of the meat as the system attempts to equalize the concentration of the solute inside and outside of the meat. However, the surface of meat is not a simple membrane but a network of protein molecules, held in intricate twisted and folded shapes and to their neighbors (and to nearby water molecules) by various chemical bonds. The salt in the brine "denatures" the protein, breaking some of the bonds so the proteins relax, creating spaces where the brine can seep in and combine with the freed water. Whatever flavors are dissolved in the brine—salts, sugars, acids, essential oils of spices and herbs—get carried in too. The net effect is a slight increase in weight, but more important, extra moisture and extra flavor suffusing the meat as it cooks. As long as you don't overcook it, the result is meat that is moister and more flavorful than the same meat cooked with the same seasonings in dry form.

Garlic Mashed Potatoes

■ *Serves 4*

Mashed potatoes flavored with garlic became a restaurant cliché in the 1990s, but they never would have caught on if they weren't so good. I first learned to make them from Julia Child's Mastering the Art of French Cooking, Volume 1, *cooking the garlic by blanching it and simmering it in milk (see Variation). Later, when I learned to roast whole heads of garlic, I used that method exclusively. Now I am wavering and leaning toward a third method, simmering the whole peeled cloves in olive oil, which gives a bonus of garlic-flavored oil. Any one of these techniques lifts mashed potatoes out of the ordinary.*

1 large, firm head garlic

1 teaspoon olive oil

1¹/₂ pounds russet potatoes

¹/₂ teaspoon kosher salt, plus more to taste

2 to 3 tablespoons butter

¹/₄ to ¹/₂ cup milk

Freshly ground black pepper

Slice off the top quarter of the garlic, keeping the head intact. Place it cut side up in a small covered baking dish and drizzle the top with oil. (Or set it on a sheet of aluminum foil, drizzle with oil, and gather the foil up around the sides, pinching it together at the top.) Bake in a 375°F oven until soft, about 45 minutes. Let cool slightly. (The garlic can be roasted ahead of time and refrigerated for several days.)

Peel the potatoes and cut into 2-inch pieces. Place in a pot with water just to cover and add ¹/₂ teaspoon salt. Cover, bring to a boil, and simmer until tender. Drain, reserving some of the cooking water if you like. Squeeze the garlic out of the skins, add to the potatoes, and mash them both in the pot with a potato masher or a fork. Over low heat, whisk in the butter, moisten to your liking with milk and/or the potato water, and season to taste with salt and pepper. Serve promptly, or cover and keep warm.

VARIATION If you don't have time to roast the garlic, separate the garlic cloves, blanch for a few minutes in boiling water, then peel and simmer in the milk while the potatoes cook. Or separate and peel the cloves and cook them slowly at least half covered in olive oil until quite soft and golden brown. Save the garlic-flavored oil for another use.

Louisiana-Style Fish Courtbouillon

■ *Serves 4*

In classic French cooking, a court-bouillon is a clear, lightly flavored broth for poaching fish or vegetables. Like many French culinary terms, it takes on a somewhat different meaning in Louisiana—becoming a sort of fish stew with a tomato-flavored broth, usually based on a brown roux and often made with red wine.

For a really authentic courtbouillon, we can use the same kind of fish that southern cooks use. Gaspergou is the Louisiana name for a good-sized fresh-water drum (a relative of the more famous redfish as well as our white seabass) fished commercially in much of the Midwest and South. Between Americans from the South and certain Asian ethnic groups that favor fresh-water fish, there is a steady market for this fish in many parts of the West, and we import it by the ton from the Mississippi Delta. In fact, this silvery, hump-backed, blunt-nosed fish is often easier to find as whole fish than anything from local waters. However, you can certainly make this dish with local rock-fish, lingcod, cabezon, or any other white-fleshed fish.

1 white-fleshed fish such as rockfish or freshwater
  drum (gaspergou), 2 to 3 pounds

2 tablespoons oil

2 tablespoons flour

1 teaspoon whole allspice berries

1 cup diced onion

$1/2$ cup diced celery

$1/2$ cup diced green bell pepper

2 cloves garlic, minced

$1/2$ teaspoon dried thyme leaves, or 1 sprig fresh thyme

$1/4$ teaspoon dried marjoram

3 sprigs parsley

3 bay leaves

1 can (15 ounces) peeled tomatoes

WHICH BEER?
Pale lager.

1½ cups dry red wine

3 cups water

¼ teaspoon cayenne, or to taste

Kosher salt

Juice of 1 lemon

Have the fish scaled and cut crosswise into 2-inch sections; reserve the head. Heat the oil in a heavy soup pot or Dutch oven over medium heat. Add the flour and cook, stirring frequently to avoid scorching, until the roux is a rich medium brown.

Add the allspice, diced vegetables, garlic, and herbs to the pot (carefully, so as not to spatter the hot roux) and stir to coat them with the roux. Cook for another 5 minutes, until the onion softens. Meanwhile, empty the tomato can into a bowl and chop the tomatoes coarsely with a spoon, or crush them in your hand. Add to the pot with the wine, water, cayenne, and a large pinch of salt. Add the fish head, bring just to a boil, and simmer over low heat for 30 minutes.

Remove the fish head. Taste the sauce for salt and adjust if necessary. Add the lemon juice, then slide in the fish pieces and cook at a simmer until the fish is tender when probed with a fork, about 10 minutes. Serve the fish in deep plates or soup bowls, with sauce spooned over each portion.

Muffuletta

■ *Makes 4 sandwiches*

In the Italian-style delis of New Orleans, where this sandwich was born, it is usually made on a large round loaf and cut into wedges. This is not just a matter of convenience; the sandwich actually tastes better several hours after it is made, when the flavors of the garlicky olive and vegetable salad have soaked into the bread.

1 jar (16 ounces) Italian-style mixed pickled
  vegetables (giardiniera)

1/2 cup pitted green olives

1 tablespoon minced garlic

3 tablespoons olive oil

4 ounces thinly sliced dry salami

4 ounces thinly sliced deli-style ham

4 ounces thinly sliced cheese of your choice

4 soft sesame-topped sandwich rolls

WHICH BEER?
Pale lager.

Drain the vegetables and olives, and chop together into fine dice. Combine with the garlic and oil and refrigerate if not using right away.

For each sandwich, layer the meats, and then the cheese on the bottom half of a roll, then top with a generous layer of the olive salad. Wrap the sandwich tightly and store for at least 2 hours at room temperature; refrigerate if keeping longer than 3 or 4 hours.

Menu:
Louisiana Shrimp Boil

■

Shrimp Boil
Pepper Slaw
Gingery Peach Crisp

■

Pilsner, Hefeweizen

Just as a clambake consists of more than baked clams, there's more to a "shrimp boil" than boiled shrimp; it's a one-pot meal of shellfish, potatoes, onions, and sweet corn boiled in a lip-tingling blend of spices and red pepper.

A shrimp boil is a perfect occasion to buy a whole 2-kilo or 5-pound box of frozen shrimp and let it thaw overnight in the refrigerator. To minimize the time and effort of peeling, look for the biggest shrimp you can afford, 26 to 30 count per pound or larger. Head-on shrimp will give a better flavor but a lower yield of meat. Crawfish and crabs are also delicious served this way (see Variations, page 216).

To serve the boil in the traditional manner, spread a picnic table with newspapers, pile the cooked shellfish and vegetables on platters, and invite everyone to dig in, peeling the shellfish by hand and tossing the shells on the table. When you're done, just wrap all the trash in the paper.

Shrimp Boil

■ *Serves 8 to 10*

You can give your boil a Gulf Coast or a mid-Atlantic flavor depending on how you flavor the water. Cooks around Chesapeake Bay would use Old Bay Seasoning or one of its imitators, while in Louisiana the classic seasoning is Zatarain's Crab Boil, made in New Orleans. Both are variations on a typical "pickling spice" blend, which also works as a substitute with some tweaking (see Variation). The dry version of Zatarain's comes in a mesh bag that works like a tea bag and makes for easy retrieval from the pot. There is also a liquid version, which is pretty similar in taste and even more convenient.

Whatever spice base you use, the "boil" needs some form of ground red pepper—straight cayenne if you want it really hot, pure ground chile or hot paprika for a mellower taste. Don't skimp here; it takes at least a tablespoon of cayenne to flavor a couple of gallons of water, and 2 to 3 tablespoons is not too much for those who like hot flavors. Much of the pepper flavor ends up clinging to the shells rather than penetrating the meat, so you taste it more from the inevitable licking of fingers than in the shellfish meat itself. The potatoes, corn, and especially the onions catch a lot of the pepper heat as well. By the end of the meal, everyone should have a good red-pepper glow.

3 to 4 pounds headless shrimp, any size, or 4 to 5 pounds head-on shrimp

2 to 3 gallons water

¹⁄₂ cup vinegar

3-ounce bag Zatarain's Crab Boil, or 1 tablespoon Zatarain's liquid concentrate

1 to 2 tablespoons cayenne (omit if using Zatarain's concentrate)

¹⁄₃ cup kosher salt

2 lemons, quartered

2 pounds red potatoes, left whole if tiny, otherwise cut into 1¹⁄₂-inch chunks

2 pounds onions, quartered

WHICH BEER?

If there were ever a dish made for lawnmower beer, this is it. But feel free to serve hefeweizen or a maltier-tasting amber ale or dunkel; just avoid anything too hoppy.

1 head garlic, halved crosswise

8 to 10 ears sweet corn, halved

Devein the shrimp through the shells, if desired (see Technique Note). Fill a large stockpot (preferably not aluminum) with 2 to 2½ gallons of water. Add the vinegar, crab boil, cayenne, salt, and lemons and bring to a boil. Add the potatoes, onions, and garlic to the pot and return to a boil. Cook 15 minutes, then add the shrimp and corn and cook 5 minutes, or until the shrimp meat is opaque.

Remove the pot from the heat and let stand covered for 5 minutes, then drain through a colander (or lift everything out of the water with a large skimmer). Discard the lemons and spice bag and heap the shellfish and vegetables in a bowl or on a platter.

TECHNIQUE NOTE Check the shrimp before cooking to see if they need deveining. In some batches of shrimp, the "vein" (actually the intestinal tube) is nearly empty, while in others it is full and dark and should be removed. To get at the vein while leaving the shell intact, run the tip of a paring knife in under the shell along the dorsal (outer) curve, so it cuts outward through the shell, and slit the shell open almost to the tail.

VARIATION If you can't find Zatarain's, tie ½ cup (about 2 ounces) pickling spices, 1 teaspoon cloves, and 6 whole cardamom pods together in cheesecloth. Or for a Chesapeake flavor, omit the crab boil, add ¼ cup Old Bay or other Chesapeake seafood seasoning to the water, and reduce the salt to 2 tablespoons.

VARIATION Substitute 7 to 10 pounds live crawfish or 18 live blue crabs for the shrimp, adding them to the pot after the potatoes have cooked 10 minutes. Cook 15 minutes, adding the corn for the last 5 minutes. Of course, you can mix different types of shellfish, bearing in mind the timing differences. To eat boiled crawfish, grab the curled-under tail in one hand and the head in the other and twist them apart. The tail meat should come out with a good-sized dab of tasty orange fat on the exposed end; if not, or if you want to savor every bit of the crawfish flavor, the official method is to suck the juices out of the head. Crack open the underside of the tail, grasp the exposed meat in your teeth, and give the tip of the tail a pinch; the tail meat should come out in one piece.

Pepper Slaw

■ *Serves 8 to 10*

Red bell peppers offer a sweet flavor and contrasting color in this, my favorite variation on coleslaw. Stretching the dressing with a little yogurt shaves a few fat calories, but you won't miss them.

1 large head cabbage

2 large red bell peppers

¹⁄₃ cup mayonnaise

2 tablespoons plain yogurt

2 tablespoons Dijon-style mustard

Kosher salt and freshly ground black pepper to taste

Split the cabbage, remove the core, and slice as thinly as possible; you should have about 6 cups. Seed and core the peppers and slice into thin shreds as close as possible to the size of the cabbage shreds. Combine with the mayonnaise, yogurt, and mustard and let stand 30 minutes. Taste for seasoning and add salt and pepper, if needed. Refrigerate 1 hour to overnight.

Gingery Peach Crisp

■ *Serves 10*

Most of what I know about desserts I have learned from my wife Elaine Ratner and indirectly from pastry chef Jim Dodge, with whom Elaine worked on two classic cookbooks. This simple, summery dessert is based on a couple of Jim's recipes in The American Baker. *A stand mixer with a paddle attachment makes short work of preparing the crisp topping; if you don't have a mixer with a paddle, rub the butter together with the flour and sugar as if making pie dough, and when it reaches the consistency of coarse meal, gently press it together into pea-sized clumps.*

10 medium peaches, ripe but firm

2 tablespoons cornstarch

1 cup plus 3 tablespoons sugar

$\frac{1}{2}$ cup (about 3 ounces) crystallized ginger, coarsely chopped

10 tablespoons cold unsalted butter

1 cup bread flour

Preheat the oven to 375°F. Wash and dry the peaches, but do not peel. Cut into eighths and place in a mixing bowl. Combine the cornstarch and 3 tablespoons of the sugar, add to the peaches, and toss to coat; stir in the ginger. Spread the contents of the bowl in a shallow 2½-quart baking dish.

Cut the butter into 1-inch pieces. Combine in the bowl of an electric mixer with the flour and the remaining 1 cup sugar. Mix with the paddle attachment at low speed until crumbly; stop mixing as soon as the color begins to show yellowish. Spread the topping over the fruit and bake until the topping is golden brown and the fruit is bubbling around the edges, 1 hour to 1 hour and 10 minutes. Serve warm or at room temperature, plain or with vanilla ice cream.

Shrimp or Crawfish Étouffée

■ *Serves 4*

This thick, flavorful stew of shellfish and finely diced vegetables "smothered" in spicy broth and served over rice is a standard of Louisiana Cajun cooking. All manner of meats, poultry, and shellfish can be served étouffée style, but the most common are shrimp and crayfish (or to use the only pronunciation acceptable in Louisiana, crawfish). Some versions are thicker than others; some use a roux based on oil, others butter. But they all share a few basic traits: diced onion and sweet pepper, a garnish of sliced green onions, and a hefty dose of both red and black pepper.

Crawfish are in peak season in Louisiana in late winter and spring, and from late spring into fall on the West Coast, and some well-stocked fish markets carry the live critters in season. Cooked and peeled tail meat is available from Louisiana fresh in season and frozen the rest of the year, but not too many stores carry it regularly, so you may have to order it ahead of time. A far easier option for most cooks is to make shrimp étouffée, with fresh shrimp, if you can find them, or frozen. Either way, if you can get shrimp with the heads on, be sure to use the heads in the stock for the best flavor.

1$\frac{1}{2}$ **pounds raw shrimp (any size)**

$\frac{1}{2}$ **cup sliced yellow or green onion**

2$\frac{1}{2}$ **cups water**

1 **tablespoon kosher salt**

$\frac{1}{2}$ **teaspoon freshly ground black pepper**

$\frac{1}{2}$ **teaspoon freshly ground white pepper**

$\frac{1}{4}$ **teaspoon paprika**

$\frac{1}{4}$ **teaspoon cayenne**

5 **tablespoons butter**

$\frac{3}{4}$ **cup finely diced onion**

$\frac{1}{2}$ **cup finely diced celery**

WHICH BEER?

Pale lager, Märzen, or not-too-hoppy amber ale.

$^1\!/_2$ cup finely diced bell pepper (red, yellow, green, or a combination)

2 tablespoons minced garlic

$^1\!/_4$ teaspoon dried thyme

$^1\!/_4$ teaspoon dried basil

$^1\!/_4$ cup flour

$^3\!/_4$ teaspoon kosher salt, or to taste

$^1\!/_3$ cup sliced green onion tops

■

4 cups cooked long-grain white rice

Peel and devein the shrimp; reserve the shells. Combine the shells, sliced onion (the white parts of the green onions are fine for this purpose), and water in a saucepan. Bring to a boil, reduce to a simmer, and cook 15 to 20 minutes. Meanwhile, place the shrimp in a bowl, sprinkle with half the kosher salt, let stand 1 minute, then cover with cold water. Drain, rinse, repeat, and let drain in a colander. Combine the black pepper, white pepper, paprika, and cayenne.

Melt the butter in a cast iron skillet over medium-high heat. When it just begins to brown, add the onion, celery, and bell pepper. Cook, stirring frequently, until the onion begins to brown. Add the garlic, dried herbs, and 1 teaspoon of the pepper blend. Cook 1 minute, then stir in the flour. Cook, stirring and scraping the pan constantly, until the flour begins to darken. Strain the shrimp stock into a heatproof container and add 2 cups to the skillet along with the salt. Reduce the heat and cook, stirring, until the sauce settles down to a simmer. Taste for seasoning and adjust if necessary with more salt or more of the pepper blend.

Add the shrimp to the skillet, cover, and cook over low heat, stirring once or twice, until the shrimp are opaque, 7 to 10 minutes. Stir in the green onion tops and serve over rice.

VARIATION If using live crawfish, boil them in plain salted water or with spices as in Shrimp Boil (page 215), and when cool peel the tails. Use the heads and tail shells to flavor the broth, and taste the sauce before adding any salt. Add the meat (or cooked meat if you buy it that way) to the finished sauce just to reheat.

TECHNIQUE NOTE I'm not really sure about the chemistry here, but I think the salt-leaching process in the first step washes away some of the broken-down proteins on the surface of the shrimp; because the shrimp are salted very briefly, only a tiny bit of salt soaks into the meat. However it works, I find it really improves the flavor and texture, especially of frozen shrimp.

Winter Warmers: Strong and Spiced Ales

■

Strong (as in higher-alcohol) beers have always held a certain fascination for homebrewers and craft brewers alike. Some of it must be a reaction to America's history of watery commercial beers (although the latter are not necessarily low in alcohol; see page 7). Mostly, using a lot more malt gives a brew with a lot more flavor and body, and as a result these beers seem more appropriate in cold weather, when you might want a beer to fortify rather than simply refresh.

Drawing on Old World models from Scottish "wee heavy" to Belgian tripel and Bavarian doppelbock, many West Coast craft brewers make one or more seasonal high-gravity beers for winter consumption. Some of these are simply scaled-up versions of the brewery's other ales; to my taste, the best are those that emphasize malty and fruity character without going overboard on hops. (Deschutes Jubelale is a particularly yummy example of this approach.)

Other seasonal ales are spiced ales in the English wassail tradition. Anchor Brewing's Our Special Ale has featured a new recipe each year since the 1970's with a warming blend of spices in the pumpkin-pie range. It's typically released in mid-November, just in time for Thanksgiving, and indeed its spicy flavors work well with the sweetish and spicy trimmings of a typical Thanksgiving dinner.

While it is not necessarily pitched as a seasonal ale, I think of Imperial stout as a winter beer. This is an especially strong (up to 9 percent alcohol by volume), thick, somewhat sweet stout, in a style originally brewed in England for export to the Russian tsars. I like it as an after-dinner drink, sipped from a small glass like port, preferably near a fireplace. Grant's Imperial Stout, the pioneer of the style in the West, is worth seeking out on tap. For a bottled version, look for Old Rasputin from North Coast Brewing.

At the top end of the beer strength spectrum is barley wine, or "barleywine-style ale" as it is called to satisfy the regulators. To reach alcohol levels of 9 to 11 percent requires several strains of yeast and long fermentation, providing especially complex aromas. Again, these beers are more for sipping alone than for serving at the table, though they can go nicely with dessert, especially chocolate.

Menu: Thanksgiving Dinner

■

Leek and Potato Soup

Cider-Brined Roast Stuffed Turkey with
Giblet Gravy

Rye Bread and Apple Stuffing

Mixed Rice Jambalaya

Cranberry-Orange Relish

Maggie Klein's Squash Gratin with Garlic
and Olive Oil

■

Anchor Our Special Ale

Widmer Wildwood Cider

Your turn to host Thanksgiving? There's no need to hide the beer and serve only wine. Here is a menu that should satisfy the traditionalists but provide plenty of opportunity to show off your favorite seasonal beers. There's also enough meatless stuff here to take care of the vegetarians in the crowd. (Note that this is not a complete menu; let those folks who ask what they can contribute bring the salad, bread, and pie. Assign someone to bring wine or other beverages for the non-beer drinkers.)

If this is your first time (or even if it isn't), the following timetable may help you survive the whole process and actually feel relaxed when you sit down to dinner. The schedule assumes a 12-pound turkey stuffed with the bread stuffing; allow more time for a larger bird, or if you want to stuff the bird with the jambalaya instead of the bread stuffing (a tasty alternative).

Up to a week ahead:

■ Buy durable produce like onions, carrots, and squash. Stale bread is fine for dressing, so buy rye bread while you're at it. Don't forget the beer and cider.

■ Order now for a top-quality fresh turkey; if using frozen turkey, buy it at least 3 days ahead to give it ample time to thaw in the refrigerator (in a roasting pan to catch drips).

1 to 3 days ahead:

■ Pick up fresh turkey, preferably in a large plastic bag you can use for brining.

■ Dice the vegetables for stuffing and so on a day ahead of time and stored tightly covered in the refrigerator.

■ Make the stuffing a day ahead and refrigerate it; remove an hour or so before stuffing to let it warm up.

■ Make the leek soup up to the final addition of milk and refrigerate.

■ The only last-day shopping needs are shrimp for the jambalaya and delicate vegetables like salad greens (which you're assigning to someone else, right?). Consider IQF (individually frozen) shrimp, which you can buy ahead and thaw in any quantity you need.

8 to 24 hours ahead:

■ Brine the turkey.

■ Make stock from the giblets.

■ Dice jambalaya, stuffing, and squash gratin ingredients.

■ Make the shrimp stock.

■ If your oven is not big enough to hold both the turkey and the squash gratin, bake the gratin 1½ hours before starting the turkey, then remove it and set aside at room temperature.

3 to 4 hours before serving time:

■ Remove the turkey from the refrigerator.

■ Preheat the oven.

■ Assemble the bread stuffing.

■ Melt the shortening for basting the turkey.

■ Stuff the turkey and put it in the oven.

■ Prepare the jambalaya through adding the stock.

■ Assemble the other side dishes.

■ Set the table.

■ Chill the beverages.

45 minutes to 1 hour before serving time:

■ Warm the plates and turkey platter.

■ Monitor the turkey for doneness; remove it from the oven when done.

■ Put the side dishes into the oven to bake or finish.

■ Drain the drippings from the roasting pan; set aside to separate.

■ Make the gravy.

■ Add the rice and shrimp to the jambalaya.

■ Finish the soup.

■ Serve the soup, then carve the turkey while others help serve the side dishes.

Cider-Brined Roast Stuffed Turkey with Giblet Gravy

▦ *Serves 8 to 12*

1 fresh turkey, 12 to 15 pounds

▦

BRINE

1 gallon water

$^2/_3$ cup kosher salt

$^1/_4$ cup frozen apple juice concentrate, or 1 cup fresh apple juice

1 bay leaf

2 or 3 sprigs thyme

1 teaspoon peppercorns

▦

Water or unsalted poultry stock

Mixed Rice Jambalaya (page 230) or Rye Bread and Apple Stuffing (page 229)

3 or 4 ribs celery, cut into 4-inch lengths

3 medium carrots, cut into 4-inch lengths

2 medium onions, quartered

$^1/_4$ cup melted vegetable shortening or vegetable oil

$^1/_2$ cup dry sherry, dry white wine, or not-too-tannic red wine (optional)

4 cups poultry stock

$^1/_4$ cup flour

Kosher salt and freshly ground black pepper

Remove and discard any wire or other clamp holding the turkey legs. Remove the giblets and any excess fat from the main and neck cavities; set aside the giblets for now. Remove the kidneys, if present (inside the cavity tucked in on either side of the backbone). Rinse the bird well and drain.

Combine the brine ingredients, stirring to dissolve the salt. Place the turkey in a strong, food-grade plastic bag (the one you brought it home in is fine), pour in the brine, and gather up the bag to surround the turkey and expel all the air. Seal the bag with a twist tie, set in a large bowl or other container to catch any leaks, and refrigerate 6 hours to overnight.

At your leisure, rinse the giblets (the gizzard and heart, plus neck if you like, but not the liver), put them in a saucepan with water or stock to cover, and simmer until tender, 1 to 1½ hours. (This can be done on brining day or roasting day, whichever is more convenient.)

Have the stuffing or jambalaya ready and at room temperature.

Remove the turkey from the brine approximately 3 hours before serving time; drain, rinse, and pat dry. Line a roasting pan (disposable is fine) with celery, carrots, and onions to form a "roasting rack" and lay the turkey on top. Let stand at room temperature while you preheat the oven to 350°F.

Just before roasting, spoon the stuffing loosely into the turkey cavity, leaving at least an inch of airspace. Put another spoonful into the neck cavity. Tuck the wingtips behind the back, trapping the neck skin. Fold a piece of cheesecloth 3 or 4 layers thick to cover the turkey breast and slowly spoon enough oil or melted shortening over the cloth to saturate it. Place the turkey in the oven, legs toward the hotter part (usually the back) and roast at 350°F (325°F for larger birds) 12 to 15 minutes per pound, or until the breast and thigh meat both register 160°F. Baste once or twice during the roasting time, and remove the cheesecloth after the first hour so the breast skin will brown evenly.

While the turkey roasts, check the giblets for tenderness. When tender, dice finely; reserve the stock for gravy.

Remove the turkey from the oven and transfer to a platter or carving board. The oven is now available for final baking of side dishes. (If the stuffing is not up to 160°F, remove it from the turkey and bake it a little longer in a buttered casserole, preferably one that can go to the table.) Cover the turkey loosely with foil to keep it warm.

Strain the drippings from the roasting pan into a deep heatproof container (preferably glass); discard any loose vegetables, but leave any that are stuck to the pan for now. Add the optional wine or ½ cup stock to the roasting pan, set the pan over a stovetop burner, and bring to a boil, scraping up and dissolving the browned drippings (this is what recipes call "deglazing"). Gradually add 4 cups stock (this can include the broth from cooking the giblets), stirring to incorporate the deglazed drippings. Remove from the heat.

Spoon 3 tablespoons fat from the strained drippings into a saucepan. Heat until a pinch of flour sizzles on contact, then stir in the flour. Cook over medium heat, stirring frequently, until the mixture (roux) cooks to an even golden brown. Meanwhile, discard the remaining fat from the pan juices, either by ladling it off, by drawing the juices out from under the fat with a bulb baster, or with a gravy separator. When the roux is browned, gradually add the (strained) liquid from the roasting pan, whisking to dissolve any lumps of roux, and then stir in the defatted drippings. Add the diced giblets, taste for seasoning and correct if necessary, and simmer until the gravy is smooth and well flavored.

TECHNIQUE NOTE Carving a turkey at the table is impressive, but it's much easier to do it away from the table where there is more room. After showing off the whole turkey (oohs and ahhs), set the platter next to a cutting board, preferably one with a groove for the juices. Cut the skin where a leg lies next to the breast and pull or twist the leg away from the body; if you need to pry or twist, use the carving fork rather than the knife for leverage. Carve off good-sized pieces of drumstick and thigh meat and transfer to a second warm serving platter. Make a horizontal cut just about the wing, then a shallow cut along the ridge of the breastbone. With the fork, gently separate the whole breast half from the bone, cutting it free with the tip of the knife. Transfer the breast to the cutting board and slice crosswise, catching a bit of skin with each slice. Let the slices land like shingles for now, then slide the knife under a bunch of them and transfer to the platter. Cut off and divide the wing and add it to the platter. Cut and add any large bits left on the carcass. Decide whether there is enough on the platter for a first serving for everyone, and if so, wait until time for seconds to carve the other side.

Rye Bread and Apple Stuffing

■ *Makes enough to stuff a 12- to 15-pound turkey*

Is it stuffing or dressing? That depends on your family traditions more than where it's baked (inside the bird or outside).

8 to 10 slices (about $1/2$ pound) rye bread with caraway
  seeds (to yield 8 cups diced)

3 tablespoons olive oil, butter, or a combination

2 cups diced onion

1 cup diced celery (about 2 ribs)

2 cups peeled, diced apple (2 large apples)

Heaping teaspoon kosher salt, or to taste (see Note)

Freshly ground black pepper

About 1 cup unsalted chicken or turkey stock

1 or 2 eggs (optional)

Dice the bread; if time permits, lay the cubes out on a sheet pan to dry for several hours, or toast briefly in a low oven. Meanwhile, heat the oil in a large skillet and cook the onion and celery until the onion begins to soften. Add the apple and cook another minute or two, then combine with the bread cubes and season with salt and pepper to taste. Moisten with stock until the mixture is just wet enough to stick together, using less stock for a stuffing to be baked inside the bird and more for baking in a casserole. Add an egg or two if you like, for a richer texture.

NOTE If you will be baking the stuffing inside a brined bird, use a little less salt, as it will absorb some salt with the meat juices.

Mixed Rice Jambalaya

■ *Makes 6 cups (enough to stuff a 12- to 15-pound turkey)*

This can be served as a side dish or stuffed inside a turkey before roasting. It works with plain brown rice, a fragrant specialty brown rice such as basmati or Wehani, or one of the excellent packaged blends produced by Lundberg Farms, with or without wild rice. If you use a blend that contains black japonica rice, don't be surprised when the whole dish, including the shrimp, turns purple!

1 pound raw shrimp in the shell

4 cups unsalted poultry stock, or half water and half canned chicken broth

2 tablespoons oil

1 cup finely diced onion

1 cup finely diced celery

1 cup finely diced red or green bell pepper

1 tablespoon minced garlic

1 can (16 ounces) crushed tomatoes, with juice

4 ounces smoked ham, diced

$1/4$ teaspoon paprika

$1/4$ teaspoon freshly ground black pepper

$1/4$ teaspoon freshly ground white pepper

$1/4$ teaspoon cayenne

$1/2$ teaspoon dried thyme

$1/2$ teaspoon dried sage

2 bay leaves

$1/2$ teaspoon kosher salt (reduce if using canned broth)

2 cups long-grain brown rice or a fragrant brown rice blend

Peel the shrimp and devein if necessary; reserve the shells. Combine the shells and stock, simmer 30 minutes, and strain. Add water as needed to restore the volume to 4 cups.

Heat the oil in a heavy flameproof casserole, add the diced vegetables and garlic, and cook, stirring frequently, until the onions are soft but not browned. Add the tomatoes, ham, and seasonings and cook 10 minutes. Add the stock, taste for seasoning, and adjust if necessary (it should be quite spicy, as the rice will absorb a lot of the flavor).

Add the rice and shrimp, bring to a boil, reduce the heat, and simmer uncovered until the liquid is absorbed and the rice is done, 50 to 60 minutes. Allow to cool before using as a stuffing.

WHICH BEER?

With turkey, see page 223; on its own, your favorite lager or amber ale.

Cranberry-Orange Relish

■ *Serves 12*

I don't know who invented this or when, but it brings to mind Brillat-Savarin's aphorism "The discovery of a new dish does more for human happiness than the discovery of a star." The realization that cranberries don't have to be cooked or oversweetened to make a good accent to roast turkey was one of the greatest innovations to hit the Thanksgiving table in the twentieth century.

Pecans make a nice substitute for walnuts.

1 bag (12 ounces) cranberries

1 large orange, preferably seedless

½ cup walnut halves or pieces

1 cup sugar, or to taste

Sort the cranberries, discarding any that are soft or discolored. Wash the orange well, slice it crosswise, and remove any seeds. Combine the berries, orange slices, nuts, and ½ cup sugar in a food processor and chop to a crumbly texture. Transfer to a bowl, let stand for 30 minutes to allow the sugar to combine with the fruit, and add more sugar to taste.

Leek and Potato Soup

■ *Serves 8 to 12*

Nothing radical here, just a really good and popular soup to begin the meal. Make it with vegetable stock and you have one more thing that the vegetarians at the table can enjoy.

4 large leeks (about 2½ pounds)

3 tablespoons butter

3 pounds russet potatoes (4 large bakers)

Heaping teaspoon kosher salt, or to taste

2 cups milk

Unsalted poultry or vegetable stock or additional milk

Freshly ground white pepper

Snipped chives, for garnish

Slice the white and pale green parts of the leeks (everything that is closer to white or yellow than green) crosswise and place in a bowl of water. Pull apart the rings and swirl to remove any dirt. Lift the leeks out of the water and drain in a colander. Use the same water to wash the heavy green tops; save these for poultry or vegetable stock.

Melt the butter in a soup pot over medium-low heat. Add the leeks and cook, stirring occasionally, until wilted. Meanwhile, peel the potatoes and cut into 1-inch cubes. Add the potatoes to the pot with water to cover. Add the salt, bring just to a boil, and simmer over low heat until the potatoes and leeks are both tender. Remove from the heat and let cool. Purée the soup in a blender in batches, then strain through a coarse sieve; or better still, put the soup through the medium disk of a food mill, which purées and strains in one action. (The soup base can be made to this point up to 2 days ahead of time and refrigerated.)

Combine the soup base and milk, and add stock or more milk as needed to bring the volume up to 3 quarts. Season to taste with salt and pepper and reheat over moderate heat, stirring frequently; do not let the soup boil after adding the milk. Correct the seasoning and serve garnished with chives.

Maggie Klein's Squash Gratin with Garlic and Olive Oil

■ *Serves 12*

Years ago, after the manuscript for my first cookbook was done, my publisher hired me to test recipes for another book, on olives and olive oil. The author, Maggie Klein, went on to open the justly famous Oliveto restaurant in Oakland, and her book has gone through a couple of incarnations but is now out of print. If you can find a copy of either the original 1983 Aris Books edition of The Feast of the Olive *or the later Chronicle Books edition, jump on it.*

This remains my favorite recipe from Maggie's book, and one that I have been serving for Thanksgiving dinner just about every year since then.

5 pounds butternut or other firm orange squash

12 cloves garlic, minced

1 large bunch parsley, finely chopped

Heaping teaspoon kosher salt

Freshly ground black pepper

$1/2$ cup flour

$3/4$ cup olive oil

Preheat the oven to 350°F. Peel and seed the squash and cut it into $1/3$-inch cubes. Combine in a large bowl with the garlic and parsley. Season with salt and pepper, then sprinkle in the flour and toss until all the cubes are coated with flour.

Oil a large gratin dish or wide, shallow casserole with a little of the oil. Spread the squash mixture in the dish and drizzle the remaining oil over the squash in a crisscross fashion. Bake until the top forms a crisp, brown crust, about 2 hours.

INDEX